The Wisdom of
BUDDHA

The Wisdom of

BUDDHA

PHILOSOPHICAL
LIBRARY

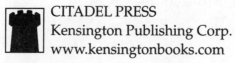

CITADEL PRESS
Kensington Publishing Corp.
www.kensingtonbooks.com

CITADEL PRESS books are published by

Kensington Publishing Corp.
850 Third Avenue
New York, NY 10022

Titles included in the Wisdom Library are published by arrangement with the Philosophical Library.

All Kensington titles, imprints, and distributed lines are available at special quantity discounts for bulk purchases for sales promotions, premiums, fund-raising, educational, or institutional use. Special book excerpts or customized printings can also be created to fit specific needs. For details, write or phone the office of the Kensington special sales manager: Kensington Publishing Corp., 850 Third Avenue, New York, NY 10022, attn: Special Sales Department, phone 1–800-221–2647.

Citadel Press and the Citadel logo are trademarks of Kensington Publishing Corp.

First Wisdom Library printing: November 2001

10 9 8 7 6 5 4 3 2 1

Printed in the United States of America

Library of Congress Control Number: 2001091761

ISBN 0-8065-2285-2

CONTENTS

PREFACE

This book needs no preface for those who are familiar with the sacred books of Buddhism. To those not familiar with the subject, it may be stated that the bulk of its contents is derived from the old Buddhist canon and concentrates on the life of Buddha and on the Buddhist doctrine.

Siddhartha Gautama, known as Buddha, the "Awakened," was the son of a ruler of ancient Northern India. The date of his birth is placed about 557 B.C. in the region of Cakyaland.

He was born a warrior prince, but at the age of twenty-nine, after having married and had a son, he decided to renounce the world. Abandoning his family and possessions, he gave himself up to asceticism and concentration of thought, under the guidance of masters of these disciplines. After seven years, he concluded that this method failed to bring him nearer to the wisdom he sought as a means of escaping rebirth into a life which he had found not worth living—so, for a time, he tried starvation and self-torture. This too, was to no avail. But suddenly, while sitting under the sacred fig tree at Bodhi Gaya, he underwent a powerful illumination and beheld the great truths he had been seeking. Henceforth, he was Buddha.

Gautama's first aim had been merely his own salvation; now, moved by pity for mankind, he resolved to bestow on others the Four Great Truths and the Eight-fold Path. He began his ministry at Benares, where he at first converted five monks who had been his companions in asceticism,

then many of the youth of the city, then a thousand Brahman priests.

He spent the remainder of his life wandering about and
preaching his new creed, which spread with extraordinary
rapidity. He died not far from his native region about the
year 477 B.C.

T.K.

The Wisdom of
BUDDHA

THE BIRTH OF THE BUDDHA

Translated from the Introduction to the Jātaka (i.47^{21})

NOW while the Future Buddha was still dwelling in the city of the Tusita gods, the "Buddha-Uproar," as it is called, took place. For there are three uproars which take place in the world,—the Cyclic-Uproar, the Buddha-Uproar, and the Universal-Monarch-Uproar. They occur as follows:—

When it is known that after the lapse of a hundred thousand years the cycle is to be renewed, the gods called Lokabyūhas, inhabitants of a heaven of sensual pleasure, wander about through the world, with hair let down and flying in the wind, weeping and wiping away their tears with their hands, and with their clothes red and in great disorder. And thus they make announcement:—

"Sirs, after the lapse of a hundred thousand years, the cycle is to be renewed; this world will be destroyed; also the mighty ocean will dry up; and this broad earth, and Sineru, the monarch of the mountains, will be burnt up and destroyed,—up to the Brahma heavens will the destruction of the world extend. Therefore, sirs, cultivate friendliness; cultivate compassion, joy, and indifference; wait on your mothers; wait on your fathers; and honor your elders among your kinsfolk."

This is called the Cyclic-Uproar.

Again, when it is known that after a lapse of a thousand years an omniscient Buddha is to arise in the world, the guardian angels of the world wander about, proclaiming:

1

"Sirs, after the lapse of a thousand years a Buddha will arise in the world."

This is called the Buddha-Uproar.

And lastly, when they realize that after the lapse of a hundred years a Universal Monarch is to arise, the terrestrial deities wander about, proclaiming:—

"Sirs, after the lapse of a hundred years a Universal Monarch is to arise in the world."

This is called the Universal-Monarch-Uproar. And these three are mighty uproars.

When of these three Uproars they hear the sound of the Buddha-Uproar, the gods of all ten thousand worlds come together into one place, and having ascertained what particular being is to be The Buddha, they approach him, and beseech him to become one. But it is not till after omens have appeared that they beseech him.

At that time, therefore, having all come together in one world, with the Catum-Mahārājas, and with the Sakka, the Suyāma, the Santusita, the Paranimmita-Vasavatti, and the Māha-Brahma of each several world, they approached the Future Buddha in the Tusita heaven, and besought him, saying,—

"Sir, it was not to acquire the glory of a Sakka, or of a Māra, or of a Brahma, or of a Universal Monarch, that you fulfilled the Ten Perfections; but it was to gain omniscience in order to save the world, that you fulfilled them. Sir, the time and fit season for your Buddhaship has now arrived."

But the Great Being, before assenting to their wish, made what is called the five great observations. He observed, namely, the time, the continent, the country, the family, and the mother and her span of life.

In the first of these observations he asked himself whether it was the right time or no. Now it is not the right time when the length of men's lives is more than a hundred thousand years. And why is it not the right time? Because mortals then forget about birth, old age, and death. And if The Buddhas, who always include in their teachings the Three Characteristics, were to attempt at such a time to discourse concerning transitoriness, misery, and the lack of substantive reality, men would not think it worth while listening to them, nor would they give them credence. Thus there would be no conversions made; and if there were no conversions, the dispensation would not conduce to salvation. This, therefore, is not the right time.

Also it is not the right time when men's lives are less than a hundred years. And why is it not the right time? Because mortals are then exceedingly corrupt; and an exhortation given to the exceedingly corrupt makes no impression, but, like a mark drawn with a stick on the surface of the water, it immediately disappears. This, therefore, also is not the right time.

But when the length of men's lives is between a hundred years and a hundred thousand years, then is it the right time. Now at that time men's lives were a hundred years; accordingly the Great Being observed that it was the right time for his birth.

Next he made the observation concerning the continent. Looking over the four continents with their attendant isles, he reflected: "In three of the continents the Buddhas are never born; only in the continent of India are they born." Thus he decided on the continent.

Next he made the observation concerning the place. "The continent of India is large," thought he, "being ten thousand leagues around. In which of its countries are The Buddhas born?" Thus he decided on the Middle Country.

The Middle Country is the country defined in the Vinaya as follows:—

"It lies in the middle, on this side of the town Kajaṅgala on the east, beyond which is Māha-Sāla, and beyond that the border districts. It lies in the middle, on this side of the river Salalavatīon the southeast, beyond which are the border districts. It lies in the middle, on this side of the town Setakannika on the south, beyond which are the border districts. It lies in the middle, on this side of the Brahmanical town Thūna on the west, beyond which are the border districts. It lies in the middle, on this side of the hill Usīraddhaja on the north, beyond which are the border districts."

It is three hundred leagues in length, two hundred and fifty in breadth, and nine hundred in circumference. In this country are born The Buddhas, the Private Buddhas, the Chief Disciples, the Eighty Great Disciples, the Universal Monarch, and other eminent ones, magnates of the warrior caste, of the Brahman caste, and the wealthy householders. "And in it is this city called Kapilavatthu," thought he, and concluded that there he ought to be born.

Then he made the observation concerning the family. "The Buddhas," thought he, "are never born into a family of the peasant caste, or of the servile caste; but into one of the warrior caste, or of the Brahman caste, whichever at the time is the higher in public estimation. The warrior caste is now the higher in public estimation. I will be born into a warrior family, and king Suddhodana shall be my father." Thus he decided on the family.

Then he made the observation concerning the mother. "The mother of a Buddha," thought he, "is never a wanton, nor a drunkard, but is one who has fulfilled the perfections through a hundred thousand cycles, and has kept the five precepts unbroken from the day of her birth. Now this queen Mahā-Māyā is such a one; and she shall be my mother."—"But what shall be her span of life?"[1] continued

[1]That is, "How long is she to live after conceiving me?" And the answer is, "Ten lunar [that is, the nine calendar] months of my mother's pregnancy, and seven days afer my birth."

he. And he perceived that it was to be ten months and seven days.

Having thus made the five great observations, he kindly made the gods the required promise, saying,—

"Sirs, you are right. The time has come for my Buddhaship."

Then, surrounded by the gods of the Tusita heaven, and dismissing all the other gods, he entered the Nandana Grove of the Tusita capital,—for in each of the heavens there is a Nandana Grove. And here the gods said, "Attain in your next existence your high destiny," and kept reminding him that he had already paved the way to it by his accumulated merit. Now it was while he was thus dwelling, surrounded by these deities, and continually reminded of his accumulated merit, that he died, and was conceived in the womb of queen Mahā-Māyā. And in order that this matter may be fully understood, I will give the whole account in due order.

It is related that at that time the Midsummer Festival had been proclaimed in the city of Kapilavatthu, and the multitude were enjoying the feast. And queen Mahā-Māyā, abstaining from strong drink, and brilliant with garlands and perfumes, took part in the festivities for the six days previous to the day of full moon. And when it came to be the day of full moon, she rose early, bathed in perfumed water, and dispensed four hundred thousand pieces of money in great largess. And decked in full gala attire, she ate of the choicest food; after which she took the eight vows, and entered her elegantly furnished chamber of state. And lying down on the royal couch, she fell asleep and dreamed the following dream:—

The four guardian angels came and lifted her up, together with her couch, and took her away to the Himalaya Mountains. There, in the Manosilā table-land, which is sixty leagues in extent, they laid her under a prodigious sal-tree, seven leagues in height, and took up their positions respectfully at one side. Then came the wives of these guardian angels, and conducted her to Anotatta Lake, and bathed her, to remove every human stain. And after clothing her with divine garments, they anointed her with perfumes and decked her with divine flowers. Not far off was Silver Hill, and in it a golden mansion. There they spread a divine couch with its head towards the east, and laid her down upon it. Now the Future Buddha had become a superb white elephant, and was wandering about at no great distance, on Gold Hill. Descending thence, he ascended Silver Hill, and approaching from the north, he plucked a white lotus with his silvery trunk, and trumpeting loudly, went into the golden mansion. And three times he walked round his mother's couch, with his right side towards it, and striking her on her right side, he seemed to enter her womb. Thus the conception took place in the Midsummer Festival.

On the next day the queen awoke, and told the dream to the king. And the king caused sixty-four eminent Brahmans to be summoned, and spread costly seats for them on ground festively prepared with green leaves, Dalbergia flowers, and so forth. The Brahmans being seated, he filled gold and silver dishes with the best of milk-porridge compounded with ghee, honey, and treacle; and covering these dishes with others, made likewise of gold and silver, he gave the Brahmans to eat. And not only with food, but with other gifts, such as new garments, tawny cows, and so forth, he satisfied them completely. And when their every desire had been satisfied, he told them the dream and asked them what would come of it?

"Be not anxious, great king!" said the Brahmans; "a child has planted itself in the womb of your queen, and it is a male child and not a female. You will have a son. And he, if he continue to live the household life, will become a Universal Monarch; but if he leave the household life and retire from the world, he will become a Buddha, and roll back the clouds of sin and folly of this world."

Now the instant the Future Buddha was conceived in the womb of his mother, all the ten thousand worlds suddenly quaked, quivered, and shook. And the Thirty-two Prognostics appeared, as follows: an immeasurable light spread through ten thousand worlds; the blind recovered their sight, as if from desire to see this his glory; the deaf received their hearing; the dumb talked; the hunchbacked became straight of body; the lame recovered the power to walk; all those in bonds were freed from their bonds and chains; the fires went out in all the hells; the hunger and thirst of the Manes was stilled; wild animals lost their timidity; diseases ceased among men; all mortals became mild-spoken; horses neighed and elephants trumpeted in a manner sweet to the ear; all musical instruments gave forth their notes without being played upon; bracelets and other ornaments jingled; in all quarters of the heavens the weather became fair; a mild, cool breeze began to blow, very refreshing to men; rain fell out of season; water burst forth from the earth and flowed in streams; the birds ceased flying through the air; the rivers checked their flowing; in the mighty ocean the water became sweet; the ground became everywhere covered with lotuses of the five different colors; all flowers bloomed, both those on land and those that grow in the water; trunk-lotuses bloomed on the trunks of trees, branch-lotuses on the branches, and vine-lotuses on the vines; on the ground, stalk-lotuses, as they are called, burst through the overlying rocks and came up by sevens; in the sky were produced others, called hanging-lotuses; a shower of flowers fell all about; celestial music was heard to play in the sky; and the whole ten thousand worlds became one mass of garlands of the utmost possible magnificence, with waving chowries, and saturated with the incense-like fragrance of flowers, and resembled a bouquet of flowers sent whirling through the air or a closely woven wreath, or a superbly decorated altar of flowers.

From the time the Future Buddha was thus conceived, four angels with swords in their hands kept guard, to ward off all harm from both the Future Buddha and the Future Buddha's mother. No lustful thought sprang up in the mind of the Future Buddha's mother; having reached the pinnacle of good fortune and of glory, she felt comfortable and well, and experienced no exhaustion of body. And within her womb she could distinguish the Future Buddha, like a white thread passed through a transparent jewel. And whereas a womb that has been occupied by a Future Buddha is like the shrine of a temple, and can never be occupied or used again, therefore it was that the mother of the Future Buddha died when he was seven days old, and was reborn in the Tusita heaven.

Now other women sometimes fall short of and sometimes run over the term of ten lunar months, and then bring forth either sitting or lying down; but not so the mother of a Future Buddha. She carries the Future Buddha in her womb for just ten months, and then brings forth while standing up. This is a characteristic of the mother of a Future Buddha. So also queen Mahā-Māyā carried the Future Buddha in her womb, as it were oil in a vessel, for ten months; and being then far gone with child, she grew desirous of going home to her relatives, and said to king Suddhodana,—

"Sire, I should like to visit my kinsfolk in their city Devadaha."

"So be it," said the king; and from Kapilavatthu to the city of Devadaha he had the road made even, and garnished it with plantain-trees set in pots, and with banners, and streamers; and, seating the queen in a golden palanquin borne by a thousand of his courtiers, he sent her away in great pomp.

Now between the two cities, and belonging to the inhabitants of both, there was a pleasure-grove of sal-trees, called Lumbini Grove. And at this particular time this grove was one mass of flowers from the ground to the topmost branches, while amongst the branches and flowers hummed swarms of bees of the five different colors, and flocks of various kinds of birds flew about warbling sweetly. Throughout the whole of Lumbini Grove the scene resembled the Cittalatā Grove in Indra's paradise, or the magnificently decorated banqueting pavilion of some potent king.

When the queen beheld it she became desirous of disporting herself therein, and the courtiers therefore took her into it. And going to the foot of the monarch sal-tree of the grove, she wished to take hold of one of its branches. And the sal-tree branch, like the tip of a well-steamed reed, bent itself down within reach of the queen's hand. Then she reached out her hand, and seized hold of the branch, and immediately her pains came upon her. Thereupon the people hung a curtain about her, and retired. So her delivery took place while she was standing up, and keeping fast hold of the sal-tree branch.

At that very moment came four pure-minded Mahā-Brahma angels bearing a golden net, and, receiving the Future Buddha on this golden net, they placed him before his mother and said,—

"Rejoice, O Queen! A mighty son has been born to you."

Now other mortals on issuing from the maternal womb are smeared with disagreeable, impure matter; but not so the Future Buddha. He issued from his mother's womb like a preacher descending from his preaching-seat, or a man coming down a stair, stretching out both hands and both feet, unsmeared by any impurity from his mother's womb, and flashing pure and spotless, like a jewel thrown upon a vesture of Benares cloth. Notwithstanding this, for the sake of honoring the Future Buddha and his mother, there came two streams of water from the sky, and refreshed the Future Buddha and his mother.

Then the Brahma angels, after receiving him on their golden net, delivered him to the four guardian angels, who received him from their hands on a rug which was made of the skins of black antelopes, and was soft to the touch, being such as is used on state occasions; and the guardian angels delivered him to men who received him on a coil of fine cloth; and the men let him out of their hands on the ground, where he stood and faced the east. There, before him, lay many thousands of worlds, like a great open court; and in them, gods and men, making offerings to him of perfumes, garlands, and so on, were saying,—

"Great Being! There is none your equal, much less your superior."

When he had in this manner surveyed the four cardinal points, and the four intermediate ones, and the zenith, and the nadir, in short, all the ten directions in order, and had nowhere discovered his equal, he exclaimed, "This is the best direction," and strode forward seven paces, followed by Mahā-Brahma holding over him the white umbrella, Suyāma bearing the fan, and other divinities having the other symbols of royalty in their hands. Then, at the seventh stride, he halted, and with a noble voice, he shouted the shout of victory, beginning,—

"The chief am I in all the world."

Now in three of his existences did the Future Buddha utter words immediately on issuing from his mother's womb:

namely, in his existence as Mahosadha; in his existence as Vessantara; and in this existence.

As respects his existence as Mahosadha, it is related that just as he was issuing from his mother's womb, Sakka, the king of the gods, came and placed in his hand some choice sandal-wood, and departed. And he closed his fist upon it, and issued forth.

"My child," said his mother, "what is it you bring with you in your hand?"

"Medicine, mother," said he.

Accordingly, as he was born with medicine in his hand, they gave him the name of Osadha-Dāraka [Medicine-Child]. Then they took the medicine, and placed it in an earthenware jar; and it was a sovereign remedy to heal all the blind, the deaf, and other afflicted persons who came to it. So the saying sprang up, "This is a great medicine, this is a great medicine!" And thus he received the name of Mahosadha [Great Medicine-Man].

Again, in the Vessantara existence, as he was issuing from his mother's womb, he stretched out his right hand, and said,—

"Pray, mother, is there anything in the house? I want to give alms."

Then, after he had completely issued forth, his mother said,—

"It's a wealthy family, my son, into which you are born;" and putting his hand in her own, she had them place in his a purse containing a thousand pieces of money.

Lastly, in this birth he shouted the shout of victory above-mentioned.

Thus in three of his existences did the Future Buddha utter words immediately on issuing from his mother's womb. And just as at the moment of his conception, so also at the moment of his birth appeared the Thirty-two Prognostics.

Now at the very time that our Future Buddha was born in Lumbini Grove there also came into existence the mother of Rāhula, and Channa the courtier, Kāludāyi the courtier, Kanthaka the king of horses, the Great Bo-tree, and the four urns full of treasure. Of these last, one was a quarter of a league in extent, another a half-league, the third three-quarters of a league, and the fourth a league. These seven[2] are called the Connate Ones.

Then the inhabitants of both cities took the Future Buddha, and carried him to Kapilavatthu.

---

[2] In making up this number the Future Buddha is to be counted as number I, and the four urns of treasure together as number 7.

THE ATTAINMENT OF BUDDHASHIP

Translated from the Introduction to the Jātaka (i.68[5])

NOW at that time there lived in Uruvelā a girl named Sujātā, who had been born in the family of the householder Senāni, in General's Town. On reaching maturity she made a prayer to a certain banyan-tree, saying, "If I get a husband of equal rank with myself, and my first-born is a son, I will make a yearly offering to you of the value of a hundred thousand pieces of money." And her prayer had been successful.

And wishing to make her offering on the day of full moon of the month Visākhā, full six years after the Great Being commenced his austerities, she first pastured a thousand cows in Latthimadhu Wood, and fed their milk to five hundred cows, and the milk of these five hundred cows to two hundred and fifty, and so on down to feeding the milk of sixteen cows to eight. This "working the milk in and in," as it is called, was done to increase the thickness and the sweetness and the strength-giving properties of the milk. And when it came to be the full-moon day of Visākhā, she resolved to make her offering, and rose up early in the morning, just when night was breaking into day, and gave orders to milk the eight cows. The calves had not come at the teats of the cows; yet as soon as new pails were put under the udders, the milk flowed in streams of its own accord. When she saw this miracle, Sujātā took the milk with her own hands and placed it in a new vessel, and herself made a fire and began to cook it. While the milk-rice was

13

cooking, immense bubbles arose, and turning to the right, went round together; but not a single drop ran over the edge, and not a particle of smoke went up from the fire-place. On this occasion the four guardian angels were present, and stood guard over the fireplace; Mahā-Brahma bore aloft the canopy of state, and Sakka raked the fire-brands together and made the fire blaze up brightly. And just as a man crushes honey out of a honey-comb that has formed around a stick, so the deities by their superhuman power collected an amount of vital sap sufficient for the sustenance of the gods and men of all the four great continents and their two thousand attendant isles, and infused it into the milk-rice. At other times, to be sure, the deities infuse this sap into each mouthful; but on the day of the attainment of the Buddhaship, and on the day of decease, they placed it in the kettle itself.

When Sujātā had seen so many miracles appear to her in one day, she said to her slave-girl Punnā,—

"Punnā, dear girl, the deity is very graciously disposed to us to-day. I have never before seen so many marvellous things happen in so short a time. Run quickly, and get everything ready at the holy place."

"Yes, my lady," replied the slave-girl, and ran in great haste to the foot of the tree.

Now that night the Future Buddha had five great dreams, and on considering their meaning reached the conclusion, "Without doubt I shall become a Buddha this very day." And when night was over, and he had cared for his person, he came early in the morning to that tree, to await the hour to go begging. And when he sat down he illumined the whole tree with his radiance.

Then came Punnā, and saw the Future Buddha sitting at the foot of the tree, contemplating the eastern quarter of the world. And when she beheld the radiance from his body lighting up the whole tree with a golden color, she became greatly excited, saying to herself, "Our deity, methinks, has come down from the tree to-day, and has seated himself, ready to receive our offering in person." And she ran in great haste, and told Sujātā of the matter.

When Sujātā heard this news, she was overjoyed; and saying, "From this day forth be to me in the room of an eldest daughter," she decked Punnā with all the ornaments appropriate to that position. And since a Future Buddha on the day he attains the Buddhaship must needs receive a golden dish worth a hundred thousand pieces of money, therefore the idea occurred to her of putting the milk-rice in a golden dish. And bringing out a golden dish that was worth a hundred thousand, she took up the cooking-vessel and began to pour out the milk-rice. All the milk-rice rolled off like water from a lotus-leaf, and exactly filled the dish. Then, covering the dish with another, which was also made of gold, and wrapping it in a cloth, she adorned herself in all her ornaments, and with the dish on her head proceeded in state to the foot of the banyan-tree. As soon as she caught sight of the Future Buddha she was exceedingly overjoyed, supposing him to be the tree-god; and as she advanced she kept constantly bowing. And taking the pot from her head, she uncovered it, and with some flower-scented water in a golden vase, drew near and took up a position close to the Future Buddha. The earthenware bowl which the Future Buddha had kept so long, and which had been given him by Ghatīkāra, the Mahā-Brahma god, at that instant disappeared; and the Future Buddha, stretching out his right hand in an attempt to find his bowl, grasped the vase of water. Next Sujātā placed the dish of milk-rice in the hand of the Great Being. Then the Great Being looked at Sujātā; and she perceived that he was a holy man, and did obeisance, and said,—

"Lord, accept my donation, and go whithersoever it seemeth to you good." And adding, "May your wishes prosper like mine own," she departed, caring no more for her golden dish worth a hundred thousand pieces of money than if it had been a dead leaf.

The Future Buddha rose from his seat and walked round the tree with his right side towards it; and taking the dish, he proceeded to the banks of the Nerañjarā and descended into its waters, just as many thousands of Future Buddhas before him had descended on the day of their complete enlightenment.—The spot where he bathed is now a place of pilgrimage named Suppatitthita, and here he deposited the dish on the bank before descending into the water.—After bathing he dressed himself in that garb of saintship which had been the dress of many hundreds of thousands of Future Buddhas before him; and sitting down with his face to the east, he made the whole of the thick, sweet milk-rice into forty-nine pellets of the size of the fruit of the single-seeded palmyra-tree, and ate it. And he took no further nourishment until the end of the seven weeks, or forty-nine days, which he spent on the throne of wisdom after he had become a Buddha. During all that time he had no other nourishment; he neither bathed, nor rinsed his mouth, nor did he ease himself; but was wholly taken up by the delights of the Trances, of the Paths, and of the Fruits.

Now when he had consumed the milk-rice, he took the golden dish; and saying, "If I am to succeed in becoming a Buddha to-day, let this dish go up-stream; but if not, let it go down-stream," he threw it into the water. And it swam, cleaving the stream, until it came to the middle of the river, and then, like a fleet horse, it ran up-stream for a distance of eighty cubits, keeping all the while in the middle of the stream. Then it dived into a whirlpool and went to the palace of the black snake-king, and hit, "click! click!"

against the dishes that had been used by the last three Buddhas, and took its place at the end of the row. When the black snake-king heard the noise, he exclaimed,—

> "But yesterday a Buddha lived,
> And now another has been born."

and so on, through several hundred laudatory verses. As a matter of only yesterday and to-day did the times of the snake-king's appearance above ground seem to him; and his body at such times towered up into the sky to a height of one and three quarters leagues.

Then the Future Buddha took his noonday rest on the banks of the river, in a grove of sal-trees in full bloom. And at nightfall, at the time the flowers droop on their stalks, he rose up, like a lion when he bestirs himself, and went towards the Bo-tree, along a road which the gods had decked, and which was eight usabhas wide.

The snakes, the fairies, the birds, and other classes of beings did him homage with celestial perfumes, flowers, and other offerings, and celestial choruses poured forth heavenly music; so that the ten thousand worlds were filled with these perfumes, garlands, and shouts of acclaim.

Just then there came from the opposite direction a grass-cutter named Sotthiya, and he was carrying grass. And when he saw the Great Being, that he was a holy man, he gave him eight handfuls of grass. The Future Buddha took the grass, and ascending the throne of wisdom, stood on the southern side and faced the north. Instantly the southern half of the world sank, until it seemed to touch the Avīci hell, while the northern half rose to the highest of the heavens.

"Methinks," said the Future Buddha, "this cannot be the place for the attainment of the supreme wisdom;" and walking round the tree with his right side towards it, he came to the western side and faced the east. Then the western half of the world sank, until it seemed to touch the Avīci hell, while the eastern half rose to the highest of the heavens. Wherever, indeed, he stood, the broad earth rose and fell, as though it had been a huge cart-wheel lying on its hub, and some one were treading on the rim.

"Methinks," said the Future Buddha, "this also cannot be the place for the attainment of supreme wisdom;" and walking round the tree with his right side towards it, he came to the northern side and faced the south. Then the northern half of the world sank, until it seemed to touch the Avīci hell, while the southern half rose to the highest of the heavens.

"Methinks," said the Future Buddha, "this also cannot be the place for the attainment of supreme wisdom;" and walking round the tree with his right side towards it, he came to the eastern side and faced the west. Now it is on the eastern side of their Bo-trees that all The Buddhas have sat cross-legged, and that side neither trembles nor quakes.

Then the Great Being, saying to himself, "This is the immovable spot on which all The Buddhas have planted themselves! This is the place for destroying passion's net!" took hold of his handful of grass by one end, and shook it out there. And straightway the blades of grass formed themselves into a seat fourteen cubits long, of such symmetry of shape as not even the most skilful painter or carver could design.

Then the Future Buddha turned his back to the trunk of the Bo-tree and faced the east. And making the mighty resolution, "Let my skin, and sinews, and bones become dry, and welcome! and let all the flesh and blood in my body dry up! but never from this seat will I stir, until I have attained the supreme and absolute wisdom!" he sat himself down cross-legged in an unconquerable position, from which not even the descent of a hundred thunder-bolts at once could have dislodged him.

At this point the god Māra, exclaiming, "Prince Siddhattha is desirous of passing beyond my control, but I will never allow it!" went and announced the news to his army, and sounding the Māra war-cry, drew out for battle. Now Māra's army extended in front of him for twelve leagues, and to the right and to the left for twelve leagues, and in the rear as far as to the confines of the world, and it was nine leagues high. And when it shouted, it made an earthquake-like roaring and rumbling over a space of a thousand leagues. And the god Māra, mounting his elephant, which was a hundred and fifty leagues high, and had the name "Girded-with-mountains," caused a thousand arms to appear on his body, and with these he grasped a variety of weapons. Also in the remainder of that army, no two persons carried the same weapon; and diverse also in their appearances and countenances, the host swept on like a flood to overwhelm the Great Being.

Now deities throughout the ten thousand worlds were busy singing the praises of the Great Being. Sakka, the king of the gods, was blowing the conch-shell Vijayuttara. (This conch, they say, was a hundred and twenty cubits long, and when once it had been filled with wind, it would sound for four months before it stopped.) The great black snake-king sang more than a hundred laudatory verses. And Mahā-Brahma stood holding aloft the white umbrella. But as Māra's army gradually drew near to the throne of wisdom, not one of these gods was able to stand his ground, but each fled straight before him. The black snake-king dived into the ground, and coming to the snake-abode, Mañjerika, which was five hundred leagues in extent, he covered his face with both hands and lay down. Sakka slung his conch-shell Vijayuttara over his back, and took up his position on the rim of the world. Mahā-Brahma left the white umbrella at the end of the world, and fled to his Brahma-abode. Not a single deity was able to stand his ground, and the Great Being was left sitting alone.

Then said Māra to his followers,—

"My friends, Siddhattha, the son of Suddhodana, is far greater than any other man, and we shall never be able to fight him in front. We will attack him from behind."

All the gods had now disappeared, and the Great Being looked around on three sides, and said to himself, "There is no one here." Then looking to the north, he perceived Māra's army coming on like a flood, and said,—

"Here is this multitude exerting all their strength and power against me alone. My mother and father are not here, nor my brother, nor any other relative. But I have these Ten Perfections, like old retainers long cherished at my board. It therefore behooves me to make the Ten Perfections my shield and my sword, and to strike a blow with them that shall destroy this strong array." And he remained sitting, and reflected on the Ten Perfections.

Thereupon the god Māra caused a whirlwind, thinking, "By this will I drive away Siddhattha." Straightway the east wind and all the other different winds began to blow; but although these winds could have torn their way through mountain-peaks half a league, or two leagues, or three leagues high, or have uprooted forest-shrubs and trees, or have reduced to powder and scattered in all directions, villages and towns, yet when they reached the Future Buddha, such was the energy of the Great Being's merit, they lost all power and were not able to cause so much as a fluttering of the edge of his priestly robe.

Then he caused a great rain-storm, saying, "With water will I overwhelm and drown him." And through his mighty power, clouds of a hundred strata, and clouds of a thousand strata arose, and also the other different kinds. And these rained down, until the earth became gullied by the torrents of water which fell, and until the floods had risen over the tops of every forest-tree. But on coming to the Great Being, this mighty inundation was not able to wet his priestly robes as much as a dew-drop would have done.

Then he caused a shower of rocks, in which immense mountain-peaks flew smoking and flaming through the sky. But on reaching the Future Buddha they became celestial bouquets of flowers.

Then he caused a shower of weapons, in which single-edged, and double-edged swords, spears, and arrows flew smoking and flaming through the sky. But on reaching the Future Buddha they became celestial flowers.

Then he caused a shower of live coals, in which live coals as red as kimsuka flowers flew through the sky. But they scattered themselves at the Future Buddha's feet as a shower of celestial flowers.

Then he caused a shower of hot ashes, in which ashes that glowed like fire flew through the sky. But they fell at the Future Buddha's feet as sandal-wood powder.

Then he caused a shower of sand, in which very fine sand flew smoking and flaming through the sky. But it fell at the Future Buddha's feet as celestial flowers.

Then he caused a shower of mud, in which mud flew smoking and flaming through the sky. But it fell at the Future Buddha's feet as celestial ointment.

Then he caused a darkness, thinking, "By this will I frighten Siddhattha, and drive him away." And the darkness became fourfold, and very dense. But on reaching the Future Buddha it disappeared like darkness before the light of the sun.

Māra, being thus unable with these nine storms of wind,

rain, rocks, weapons, live coals, hot ashes, sand, mud, and darkness, to drive away the Future Buddha, gave command to his followers, "Look ye now! Why stand ye still? Seize, kill, drive away this prince!" And, arming himself with a discus, and seated upon the shoulders of the elephant "Girded-with-mountains," he drew near the Future Buddha, and said,—

"Siddhattha, arise from this seat! It does not belong to you, but to me."

When the Great Being heard this he said,—

"Māra, you have not fulfilled the Ten Perfections in any of their three grades; nor have you made the five great donations;[1] nor have you striven for knowledge, nor for the welfare of the world, nor for enlightenment. This seat does not belong to you, but to me."

Unable to restrain his fury, the enraged Māra now hurled his discus. But the Great Being reflected on the Ten Perfections, and the discus changed into a canopy of flowers, and remained suspended over his head. Yet they say that this keen-edged discus, when at other times Māra hurled it in anger, would cut through solid stone pillars as if they had been the tips of bamboo shoots. But on this occasion it became a canopy of flowers. Then the followers of Māra began hurling immense mountain-crags, saying, "This will make him get up from his seat and flee." But the Great Being kept his thoughts on the Ten Perfections, and the crags also became wreaths of flowers, and then fell to the ground.

Now the gods meanwhile were standing on the rim of the world, and craning their necks to look, saying,—

---

[1] These are the five donations great:
The gift of treasure, gift of child,
The gift of wife, of royal rule,
And last, the gift of life and limb.
                    From the *Abhidhānappadipika*, 421.

"Ah, woe the day! The handsome form of prince Siddhattha will surely be destroyed! What will he do to save himself?"

Then the Great Being, after his assertion that the seat which Future Buddhas had always used on the day of their complete enlightenment belonged to him, continued, and said,—

"Māra, who is witness to your having given donations?"

Said Māra, "All these, as many as you see here, are my witnesses;" and he stretched out his hand in the direction of his army. And instantly from Māra's army came a roar, "I am his witness! I am his witness!" which was like to the roar of an earthquake.

Then said Māra to the Great Being,—

"Siddhattha, who is witness to your having given donations?"

"Your witnesses," replied the Great Being, "are animate beings, and I have no animate witnesses present. However, not to mention the donations which I gave in other existences, the great seven-hundred-fold donation which I gave in my Vessantara existence shall now be testified to by the solid earth, inanimate though she be." And drawing forth his right hand from beneath his priestly robe, he stretched it out towards the mighty earth, and said, "Are you witness, or are you not, to my having given a great seven-hundred-fold donation in my Vessantara existence?"

And the mighty earth thundered, "I bear you witness!" with a hundred, a thousand, a hundred thousand roars, as if to overwhelm the army of Māra.

Now while the Great Being was thus calling to mind the donation he gave in his Vessantara existence, and saying to himself, "Siddhattha, that was a great and excellent donation which you gave," the hundred-and-fifty-league-high elephant "Girded-with-mountains" fell upon his knees before the Great Being. And the followers of Māra fled away in all directions. No two went the same way, but leaving their head-ornaments and their cloaks behind, they fled straight before them.

Then the hosts of the gods, when they saw the army of Māra flee, cried out, "Māra is defeated! Prince Siddhattha has conquered! Let us go celebrate the victory!" And the snakes egging on the snakes, the birds the birds, the deities the deities, and the Brahma-angels the Brahma-angels, they came with perfumes, garlands, and other offerings in their hands to the Great Being on the throne of wisdom. And as they came,—

"The victory now hath this illustrious Buddha won!
The Wicked One, the Slayer, hath defeated been!"
Thus round the throne of wisdom shouted joyously
The bands of snakes their songs of victory for the Sage;

"The victory now hath this illustrious Buddha won!
The Wicked One, the Slayer, hath defeated been!"
Thus round the throne of wisdom shouted joyously
The flocks of birds their songs of victory for the Sage;

"The victory now hath this illustrious Buddha won!
The Wicked One, the Slayer, hath defeated been!"
Thus round the throne of wisdom shouted joyously
The bands of gods their songs of victory for the Sage;

"The victory now hath this illustrious Buddha won!
The Wicked One, the Slayer, hath defeated been!"
Thus round the throne of wisdom shouted joyously
The Brahma-angels songs of victory for the Saint.

And the remaining deities, also, throughout the ten thousand worlds, made offerings of garlands, perfumes, and ointments, and in many a hymn extolled him.

It was before the sun had set that the Great Being thus vanquished the army of Māra. And then, while the Bo-tree in homage rained red, coral-like sprigs upon his priestly robes, he acquired in the first watch of the night the knowledge of previous existences, in the middle watch of the night, the divine eye; and in the last watch of the night, his intellect fathomed Dependent Origination.

Now while he was musing on the twelve terms of Dependent Origination, forwards and backwards, round and back again, the ten thousand worlds quaked twelve times, as far as to their ocean boundaries. And when the Great Being, at the dawning of the day, had thus made the ten thousand worlds thunder with his attainment of omniscience, all these worlds became most gloriously adorned. Flags and banners erected on the eastern rim of the world let their streamers fly to the western rim of the world; likewise those erected on the western rim of the world, to the eastern rim of the world; those erected on the northern rim of the world, to the southern rim of the world; and those erected on the southern rim of the world, to the northern rim of the world; while those erected on the level of the earth let theirs fly until they beat against the Brahma-world; and those of the Brahma-world let theirs hang down to the level of the earth. Throughout the ten thousand worlds the flowering trees bloomed; the fruit trees were weighted down by their burden of fruit; trunk-lotuses bloomed on the trunks of trees; branch-lotuses on the branches of trees; vine-lotuses on the vines; hanging-lotuses in the sky; and stalk-lotuses burst through the rocks and came up by sevens. The system of ten thousand worlds was like a bouquet of flowers sent whirling through the air, or like a thick carpet of flowers; in the intermundane spaces the eight-thousand-league-long hells, which not even the light of seven suns had formerly been able to illumine, were now flooded with radiance; the eighty-four-thousand-league-deep ocean became sweet to the taste; the rivers checked their flowing; the blind from birth received their sight; the deaf from birth their hearing; the cripples from birth the use of their limbs; and the bonds and fetters of captives broke and fell off.

When thus he had attained to omniscience, and was the centre of such unparalleled glory and homage, and so many prodigies were happening about him, he breathed forth that solemn utterance which has never been omitted by any of The Buddhas:—

"Through birth and rebirth's endless round,
Seeking in vain, I hastened on,
To find who framed this edifice.
What misery!—birth incessantly!

"O builder! I've discovered thee!
This fabric thou shalt ne'er rebuild!
Thy rafters all are broken now,
And pointed roof demolished lives!
This mind has demolition reached,
And seen the last of all desire!"

The period of time, therefore, from the existence in the Tusita Heaven to this attainment of omniscience on the throne of wisdom, constitutes the Intermediate Epoch.

FIRST EVENTS AFTER THE ATTAINMENT

Translated from the Mahā-Vagga, and
constituting the opening sections.

Hail to that Blessed One, that Saint, and
Supreme Buddha!

AT that time The Buddha, The Blessed One, was dwelling at Uruvelā at the foot of the Bo-tree on the banks of the river Nerañjarā, having just attained the Buddhaship. Then The Blessed One sat cross-legged for seven days together at the foot of the Bo-tree experiencing the bliss of emancipation.

Then The Blessed One, during the first watch of the night, thought over Dependent Origination both forward and back:—

On ignorance depends karma;
On karma depends consciousness;
On consciousness depend name and form;
On name and form depend the six organs of sense;
On the six organs of sense depends contact;
On contact depends sensation;
On sensation depends desire;
On desire depends attachment;
On attachment depends existence;
On existence depends birth;
On birth depend old age and death, sorrow, lamentation, misery, grief, and despair.

27

Thus does this entire aggregation of misery arise. But on the complete fading out and cessation of ignorance ceases karma; on the cessation of karma ceases consciousness; on the cessation of consciousness cease name and form; on the cessation of name and form cease the six organs of sense; on the cessation of the six organs of sense ceases contact; on the cessation of contact ceases sensation; on the cessation of sensation ceases desire; on the cessation of desire ceases attachment; on the cessation of attachment ceases existence; on the cessation of existence ceases birth; on the cessation of birth cease old age and death, sorrow, lamentation, misery, grief, and despair. Thus does this entire aggregation of misery cease.

Then The Blessed One, concerning this, on that occasion, breathed forth this solemn utterance,—

"When to the strenuous, meditative Brahman
There come to light the elements of being,
Then vanish all his doubts and eager questions,
What time he knows THE ELEMENTS HAVE CAUSES."

Then The Blessed One, during the middle watch of the night, thought over Dependent Origination both forward and back:—On ignorance depends karma.... Thus does this entire aggregation of misery arise. But on the complete fading out and cessation of ignorance ceases karma.... Thus does this entire aggregation of misery cease.

Then The Blessed One, concerning this, on that occasion, breathed forth this solemn utterance,—

"When to the strenuous, meditative Brahman
There come to light the elements of being,
Then vanish all his doubts and eager questions,
What time he knows HOW CAUSES HAVE AN ENDING."

Then The Blessed One, during the last watch of the night, thought over Dependent Origination both forward and back:—On ignorance depends karma. . . . Thus does this entire aggregation of misery arise. But on the complete fading out and cessation of ignorance ceases karma. . . . Thus does this entire aggregation of misery cease.

Then The Blessed One, concerning this, on that occasion, breathed forth this solemn utterance,—

> "When to the strenuous, meditative Brahman
> There come to light the elements of being,
> Then scattereth he the hordes of Māra's army;
> Like to the sun that lightens all the heavens."

End of the account of what took place under the Bo-tree.

Then The Blessed One, after the lapse of seven days, arose from that state of exalted calm, and leaving the foot of the Bo-tree, drew near to where the Ajapāla (that is, the Goatherd's) banyan-tree was; and having drawn near, he sat cross-legged at the foot of the Ajapāla banyan-tree for seven days together, experiencing the bliss of emancipation.

Then a certain Brahman, who was of a proud and contemptuous disposition, drew near to where The Blessed One was; and having drawn near, he exchanged greetings with The Blessed One. And having passed with him the greetings of friendship and civility, he stood respectfully at one side. And standing respectfully at one side, the Brahman spoke to The Blessed One as follows:—

"Gotama, what is it constitutes a Brahman? and what are the Brahman-making qualities?"

Then The Blessed One, concerning this, on that occasion, breathed forth this solemn utterance,—

"The Brahman who his evil traits hath banished,
Is free from pride, is self-restrained and spotless,
Is learned, and the holy life hath followed,
'T is he alone may claim the name of Brahman;
With things of earth he hath no point of contact."

End of the account of what took place under the Ajapāla-tree.

Then The Blessed One, after the lapse of seven days, arose from that state of exalted calm, and leaving the foot of the Ajapāla banyan-tree, drew near to where the Mucalinda tree was; and having drawn near, he sat cross-legged at the foot of the Mucalinda tree for seven days together, experiencing the bliss of emancipation.

Now at that time a great cloud appeared out of season, and for seven days it was rainy, cloudy weather, with a cold wind. Then issued Mucalinda, the serpent-king, from his abode, and enveloping the body of The Blessed One seven times with his folds, spread his great hood above his head, saying,—

"Let neither cold nor heat, nor gnats, flies, wind, sunshine, nor creeping creatures come near The Blessed One!"

Then, when seven days had elapsed, and Mucalinda, the serpent-king, knew that the storm had broken up, and that the clouds had gone, he unwound his coils from the body of The Blessed One. And changing his natural appearance into that of a young man, he stood before The Blessed One, and with his joined hands to his forehead did reverence to The Blessed One.

Then the Blessed One, concerning this, on that occasion, breathed forth this solemn utterance,—

"How blest the happy solitude
Of him who hears and knows the truth!
How blest is harmlessness towards all,
And self-restraint towards living things!
How blest from passion to be free,
All sensuous joys to leave behind!
Yet far the highest bliss of all
To quit th' illusion false—'I am.'"

End of the account of what took place under Mucalinda-tree.

THE BUDDHA'S DAILY HABITS

Translated from the Sumaṅgala-Vilāsinī (i.45[10]),
Buddhaghosa's Commentary on the Dīgha-Nikāya

HABITS are of two kinds, the profitable, and the unprofitable. Of these, the unprofitable habits of The Blessed One had been extirpated by his attainment of saintship at the time he sat cross-legged under the Bo-tree. Profitable habits, however, remained to The Blessed One.

These were fivefold: his before-breakfast habits; his after-breakfast habits; his habits of the first watch of the night; his habits of the middle watch of the night; his habits of the last watch of the night.

His before-breakfast habits were as follows:—

The Blessed One would rise early in the morning, and when, out of kindness to his body-servant[1] and for the sake of bodily comfort, he had rinsed his mouth and otherwise cared for his person, he would sit retired until it was time to go begging. And when it came time, he would put on his tunic, girdle, and robes, and taking his bowl, he would enter the village or the town for alms. Sometimes he went alone, sometimes surrounded by a congregation of priests; sometimes without anything especial happening, sometimes with the accompaniment of many prodigies.

While, namely, the Lord of the World is entering for alms, gentle winds clear the ground before him; the clouds let fall drops of water to lay the dust in his pathway, and then be-

---

[1]In order to give him a chance to acquire merit by waiting on a Buddha.

come a canopy over him; other winds bring flowers and scatter them in his path; elevations of ground depress themselves, and depressions elevate themselves; wherever he places his foot, the ground is even and pleasant to walk upon, or lotus-flowers receive his tread. No sooner has he set his right foot within the city-gate than the rays of six different colors which issue from his body race hither and thither over palaces and pagodas, and deck them, as it were, with the yellow sheen of gold, or with the colors of a painting. The elephants, the horses, the birds, and other animals give forth melodious sounds; likewise the tom-toms, lutes, and other musical instruments, and the ornaments worn by the people.

By these tokens the people would know, "The Blessed One has now entered for alms;" and in their best tunics and best robes, with perfumes, flowers, and other offerings, they issue forth from their houses into the street. Then, having zealously paid homage to The Blessed One with the perfumes, flowers, and other offerings, and done him obeisance, some would implore him, "Reverend Sir, give us ten priests to feed;" some, "Give us twenty;" and some, "Give us a hundred priests." And they would take the bowl of The Blessed One, and prepare a seat for him, and zealously show their reverence for him by placing food in the bowl.

When he had finished his meal, The Blessed One, with due consideration for the different dispositions of their minds, would so teach them the Doctrine that some would become established in the refuges, some in the five precepts, some would become converted, some would attain to the fruit of either once returning, or of never returning, while some would become established in the highest fruit, that of saintship, and would retire from the world. Having shown this kindness to the multitude, he would rise from his seat, and return to the monastery.

On his arrival there, he would take his seat in a pavilion, on the excellent Buddha-mat which had been spread for him, where he would wait for the priests to finish their meal. When the priests had finished their meal, the body-servant would announce the fact to The Blessed One. Then The Blessed One would enter the perfumed chamber.

These, then, were his before-breakfast habits.

Then The Blessed One, having thus finished his before-breakfast duties, would first sit in the perfumed chamber, on a seat that had been spread for him by his body-servant, and would wash his feet. Then, taking up his stand on the landing of the jeweled staircase which led to the perfumed chamber, he would exhort the congregation of the priests, saying,—

"O priests, diligently work out your salvation; for not often occur the appearance of a Buddha in the world and existence among men and the propitious moment and retirement from the world and the opportunity to hear the true Doctrine."

At this point some would ask The Blessed One for exercises in meditation, and The Blessed One would assign them exercises suited to their several characters. Then all would do obeisance to The Blessed One, and go to the places where they were in the habit of spending the night or the day—some to the forest, some to the foot of trees, some to the hills, and so on, some to the heaven of the Four Great Kings, . . . and some to Vasavatti's heaven.

Then The Blessed One, entering the perfumed chamber, would, if he wished, lie down for a while, mindful and conscious, and on his right side after the manner of a lion. And secondly, his body being now refreshed, he would rise, and gaze over the world. And thirdly, the people of the village or town near which he might be dwelling, who had given him breakfast, would assemble after breakfast at the monastery, again in their best tunics and their best robes, and with perfumes, flowers, and other offerings.

Thereupon The Blessed One, when his audience had assembled, would approach in such miraculous manner as was fitting; and taking his seat in the lecture-hall, on the excellent Buddha-mat which had been spread for him, he would teach the Doctrine, as suited the time and occasion. And when he perceived it was time, he would dismiss the audience, and the people would do obeisance to The Blessed One, and depart.

These were his after-breakfast habits.

When he had thus finished his after-breakfast duties, he would rise from the excellent Buddha-seat, and if he desired to bathe, he would enter the bath-house, and cool his limbs with water made ready by his body-servant. Then the body-servant would fetch the Buddha-seat, and spread it in the perfumed chamber. And The Blessed One, putting on a tunic of double red cloth, and binding on his girdle, and throwing his upper robe over his right shoulder, would go thither and sit down, and for a while remain solitary, and plunged in meditation. After that would come the priests from here and from there to wait on The Blessed One. And some would propound questions, some would ask for exercises in meditation, and some for a sermon; and in granting their desires The Blessed One would complete the first watch of the night.

These were his habits of the first watch of the night.

And now, when The Blessed One had finished his duties of the first watch of the night, and when the priests had done him obeisance and were departing, the deities throughout the entire system of ten thousand worlds would seize the opportunity to draw near to The Blessed One and ask him any questions that might occur to them, even such as were but four syllables long. And The Blessed One in answering their questions would complete the middle watch of the night.

These were his habits of the middle watch of the night.

The last watch of the night he would divide into three parts, and as his body would be tired from so much sitting since the morning, he would spend one part in pacing up and down to free himself from the discomfort. In the second part he would enter the perfumed chamber, and would lie down mindful and conscious, and on his right side after the manner of a lion. In the third part he would rise, and taking his seat, he would gaze over the world with the eye of a Buddha, in order to discover any individual who, under some former Buddha, with alms-giving, or keeping the precepts, or other meritorious deeds, might have made the earnest wish.

These were his habits of the last watch of the night.

THE DEATH OF THE BUDDHA

Translated from the Mahā-Parinibbāna-Sutta
(v. and vi.) of the Dīgha-Nikāya

THEN The Blessed One addressed the venerable Ananda:—
"Let us go hence, Ananda. To the further bank of the
Hiraññavatī river, and to the city of Kusinārā and the sal-
tree grove Upavattana of the Mallas will we draw near."

"Yes, Reverend Sir," said the venerable Ananda to The
Blessed One in assent.

Then The Blessed One, accompanied by a large congregation of priests, drew near to the further bank of the
Hiraññavatī river, and to the city of Kusinārā and the sal-
tree grove Upavattana of the Mallas; and having drawn
near, he addressed the venerable Ananda:—

"Be so good, Ananda, as to spread me a couch with its
head to the north between twin sal-trees. I am weary, Ananda,
and wish to lie down."

"Yes, Reverend Sir," said the venerable Ananda to The
Blessed One in assent, and spread the couch with its head to
the north between twin sal-trees. Then The Blessed One lay
down on his right side after the manner of a lion, and placing foot on foot, remained mindful and conscious.

Now at that time the twin sal-trees had completely burst
forth into bloom, though it was not the flowering season;
and the blossoms scattered themselves over the body of The
Tathāgata,[1] and strewed and sprinkled themselves in wor-

---

[1] Tathāgata is a term most commonly used by The Buddha in referring
to himself. Its meaning, like that of its Jaina equivalent *Tatthagaya*, possibly

ship of The Tathāgata. Also heavenly Erythrina flowers fell from the sky; and these scattered themselves over the body of The Tathāgata, and strewed and sprinkled themselves in worship of The Tathāgata. Also heavenly sandal-wood powder fell from the sky; and this scattered itself over the body of The Tathāgata, and strewed and sprinkled itself in worship of The Tathāgata. And music sounded in the sky in worship of The Tathāgata, and heavenly choruses were heard to sing in worship of The Tathāgata.

Then The Blessed One addressed the venerable Ananda:—

"The twin sal-trees, Ananda, have completely burst forth into bloom, though it is not the flowering season; and the blossoms have scattered themselves over the body of The Tathāgata, and have strewn and sprinkled themselves in worship of The Tathāgata. Also heavenly Erythrina flowers have fallen from the sky; and these have scattered themselves over the body of The Tathāgata, and have strewn and sprinkled themselves in worship of The Tathāgata. Also heavenly sandal-wood powder has fallen from the sky; and this has scattered itself over the body of The Tathāgata, and has strewn and sprinkled itself in worship of The Tathāgata. Also music is sounding in the sky in worship of The Tathāgata, and heavenly choruses are heard to sing in worship of The Tathāgata. But it is not by all this, Ananda, that The Tathāgata is honored, esteemed, revered, worshiped, or venerated; but the priest, Ananda, or the priestess, or the lay disciple, or the female lay disciple, who shall fulfil all the greater and lesser duties, conducting himself with propriety and in accordance with the precepts, by him is The

is, "He who has arrived there (tatra or tattha), i.e. to emancipation or Nirvana." See "Sacred Books of the East," vol. xiii., p. 82. [Chalmers, "Journal of the Royal Asiatic Society," 1898, p. 113, takes it as "One who has come at the real truth."]

Tathāgata honored, esteemed, revered, and worshiped with the best of worship. Accordingly, Ananda, train yourselves, and fulfil all the greater and lesser duties, and conduct yourselves with propriety and in accordance with the precepts."

Now at that time the venerable Upavāna was standing in front of The Blessed One, and fanning him. Then The Blessed One was harsh to the venerable Upavāna, saying,—"Step aside, O priest; stand not in front of me."

Then it occurred to the venerable Ananda as follows:—"Here, this venerable Upavāna has for a long time been the body-servant of The Blessed One, and kept himself at his beck and call; yet, although his last moments are near, The Blessed One is harsh to the venerable Upavāna, saying, 'Step aside, O priest; stand not in front of me.' What, pray, was the reason, and what was the cause, that The Blessed One was harsh to the venerable Upavāna, saying, 'Step aside, O priest; stand not in front of me'?"

Then the venerable Ananda spoke to The Blessed One as follows:—

"Reverend Sir, here this venerable Upavāna has for a long time been the body-servant of The Blessed One, and kept himself at his beck and call; yet, although his last moments are near, The Blessed One is harsh to the venerable Upavāna, saying, 'Step aside, O priest; stand not in front of me.' Reverend Sir, what, pray, was the reason, and what was the cause, that The Blessed One was harsh to the venerable Upavāna, saying, 'Step aside, O priest; stand not in front of me'?"

"Ananda, almost all the deities throughout ten worlds have come together to behold The Tathāgata. For an extent, Ananda, of twelve leagues about the city Kusinārā and the sal-tree grove Upavattana of the Mallas, there is not a spot of ground large enough to stick the point of a hair into, that is not pervaded by powerful deities. And these deities, Ananda, are angered, saying, 'From afar have we come to behold The Tathāgata, for but seldom, and on rare occasions, does a Tathāgata, a saint, and Supreme Buddha arise in the world; and now, to-night, in the last watch, will The Tathagata pass into Nirvana; but this powerful priest stands in front of The Blessed One, concealing him, and we have no chance to see The Tathāgata, although his last moments are near.' Thus, Ananda, are these deities angered."

"What are the deities doing, Reverend Sir, whom The Blessed One perceives?"

"Some of the deities, Ananda, are in the air with their minds engrossed by earthly things, and they let fly their hair and cry aloud, and stretch out their arms and cry aloud, and fall headlong to the ground and roll to and fro, saying, 'All too soon will The Blessed One pass into Nirvana; all too soon will The Happy One pass into Nirvana; all too soon will The Light of the World vanish from sight!' Some of the deities, Ananda, are on the earth with their minds engrossed by earthly things, and they let fly their hair and cry aloud, and stretch out their arms and cry aloud, and fall headlong on the ground and roll to and fro, saying, 'All too soon will The Blessed One pass into Nirvana; all too soon will The Happy One pass into Nirvana; all too soon will The Light of the World vanish from sight.' But those deities which are free from passion, mindful and conscious, bear it patiently, saying, 'Transitory are all things. How is it possible [that whatever has been born, has come into being, and is organized and perishable, should not perish? That condition is not possible.]' "

Then the venerable Ananda entered the monastery, and, leaning against the bolt of the door, he wept, saying,—

"Behold, I am but a learner and not yet perfect, and my

Teacher is on the point of passing into Nirvana, he who was so compassionate to me."

Then The Blessed One addressed the priests:—

"Where, O priests, is Ananda?"

"Reverend Sir, the venerable Ananda has entered the monastery, and leaning against the bolt of the door, he weeps, saying, 'Behold, I am but a learner, and not yet perfect, and my Teacher is on the point of passing into Nirvana, he who was so compassionate to me.'"

Then The Blessed One addressed a certain priest, saying,—

"Go, O priest, and say to the venerable Ananda from me, 'The Teacher calleth thee, brother Ananda.'"

"Yes, Reverend Sir," said the priest to The Blessed One in assent, and drew near to where the venerable Ananda was; and having drawn near, he spoke to the venerable Ananda as follows:—

"The Teacher calleth thee, brother Ananda."

"Yes, brother," said the venerable Ananda to the priest in assent, and drew near to where The Blessed One was; and having drawn near and greeted The Blessed One, he sat down respectfully at one side. And the venerable Ananda being seated respectfully at one side, The Blessed One spoke to him as follows:—

"Enough, Ananda, do not grieve, nor weep. Have I not already told you, Ananda, that it is in the very nature of all things near and dear unto us that we must divide ourselves from them, leave them, sever ourselves from them? How is it possible, Ananda, that whatever has been born, has come into being, is organized and perishable, should not perish? That condition is not possible. For a long time, Ananda, have you waited on The Tathāgata with a kind, devoted, cheerful, single-hearted, unstinted service of body, with a kind, devoted, cheerful, single-hearted, unstinted service of

voice, with a kind, devoted, cheerful, single-hearted, unstinted service of mind. You have acquired much merit,
Ananda; exert yourself, and soon will you be free from all
depravity."

Then The Blessed One addressed the priests:—

"Priests, of all those Blessed Ones who aforetime were
saints and Supreme Buddhas, all had their favorite body-
servants, just as I have now my Ananda. And, priests, of all
those Blessed Ones who in the future shall be saints and
Supreme Buddhas, all will have their favorite body-
servants, just as I have now my Ananda. Wise, O priests, is
Ananda—he knows when it is a fit time to draw near to see
The Tathāgata, whether for the priests, for the priestesses,
for the lay disciples, for the female lay disciples, for the
king, for the king's courtiers, for the leaders of heretical
sects, or for their adherents.

"Ananda, O priests, has four wonderful and marvellous
qualities. And what are the four? O priests, if an assembly
of priests draw near to behold Ananda, it is delighted with
beholding him, and if then Ananda hold a discourse on the
Doctrine, it is also delighted with the discourse; and when
Ananda, O priests, ceases to speak, the assembly of priests
is still unsated. O priests, if an assembly of priestesses . . .
an assembly of lay disciples . . . an assembly of female lay
disciples draw near to behold Ananda, it is delighted with
beholding him; and if then Ananda hold a discourse on the
Doctrine, it is also delighted with the discourse; and when
Ananda, O priests, ceases to speak, the assembly of female
lay disciples is still unsated.

"A Universal Monarch, O priests, has four wonderful
and marvellous qualities. And what are the four? O priests,
if an assembly of men of the warrior caste . . . an assembly of men of the Brahman caste . . . an assembly of house-

holders . . . an assembly of monks draw near to behold the Universal Monarch, it is delighted with beholding him; and if then the Universal Monarch hold a discourse, it is also delighted with the discourse; and when the Universal Monarch, O priests, ceases to speak, the assembly of monks is still unsated.

"In exactly the same way, O priests, Ananda has four wonderful and marvellous qualities. O priests, if an assembly of priests . . . an assembly of priestesses . . . an assembly of lay disciples . . . an assembly of female lay disciples draw near to behold Ananda, it is delighted with beholding him; and if then Ananda hold a discourse on the Doctrine, it is also delighted with the discourse; and when Ananda, O priests, ceases to speak, the assembly of female lay disciples is still unsated. These, O priests, are the four wonderful and marvellous qualities possessed by Ananda."

When The Blessed One had thus spoken, the venerable Ananda spoke to him as follows:—

"Reverend Sir, let not The Blessed One pass into Nirvana in this wattel-and-daub town, this town of the jungle, this branch village. For there are other great cities, Reverend Sir, to wit, Campā, Rājagaha, Sāvatthi, Sāketa, Kosambī, and Benares. Let The Blessed One pass into Nirvana in one of them. In them are many wealthy men of the warrior caste, many wealthy men of the Brahman caste, and many wealthy householders who are firm believers in The Tathāgata, and they will perform the funeral rites for The Tathāgata."

"O Ananda, say not so! O Ananda, say not so, that this is a wattel-and-daub town, a town of the jungle, a branch village. There was once, Ananda, a king called Sudassana the Great, who was a Universal Monarch, a virtuous king of justice, a victorious ruler of the four quarters of the earth, possessing a secure dominion over his territory, and owning the seven precious gems.[2] This city Kusinārā, Ananda, was the capital of king Sudassana the Great, and had then the name of Kusāvatī. From the east to the west it was twelve leagues in length, and from the north to the south it was seven leagues in breadth. Kusāvatī, the capital, Ananda, was prosperous and flourishing, populous and thronging with people, and well provided with food. As Alakamandā, the capital of the gods, Ananda, is prosperous and flourishing, populous and thronging with gods, and is well provided with food, in exactly the same way, Ananda, Kusāvatī, the capital, was prosperous and flourishing, populous and thronging with people, and well provided with food. Kusāvatī, the capital, Ananda, was neither by day nor night without the ten noises,—to wit, the noise of elephants, the noise of horses, the noise of chariots, the noise of drums, the noise of labors, the noise of lutes, the noise of song, the noise of cymbals, the noise of gongs, and the tenth noise of people crying, 'Eat ye, and drink!'

"Go thou, Ananda, and enter the city Kusinārā, and announce to the Kusinārā-Mallas:—

" 'To-night, O ye Vāsetthas, in the last watch, The Tathāgata will pass into Nirvana. Be favorable, be favorable, O ye Vāsetthas, and suffer not that afterwards ye feel remorse, saying, "The Tathāgata passed into Nirvana while in our borders, but we did not avail ourselves of the opportunity of being present at the last moments of The Tathāgata.' "

"Yes, Reverend Sir," said the venerable Ananda to The Blessed One in assent; and putting on his tunic, and taking his bowl and his robes, he went to Kusinārā with another member of the Order.

Now at that time the Kusinārā-Mallas were assembled

[2]The wheel of empire, the elephant, the horse, the gem, the empress, the treasurer, and the crown-prince.

together in the town-hall on some matter of business. And
the venerable Ananda drew near to the town-hall of the
Kusinārā-Mallas; and having drawn near, he made announcement to the Kusinārā-Mallas, as follows:—

"To-night, O ye Vasetthas, in the last watch, The Tathāgata will pass into Nirvana. Be favorable, be favorable, O ye
Vasetthas, and suffer not that afterwards ye feel remorse,
saying, 'The Tathāgata passed into Nirvana while in our
borders, but we did not avail ourselves of the opportunity
of being present at the last moments of The Tathāgata.'"

The Mallas, on hearing this speech of the venerable
Ananda, and their children and their daughters-in-law and
their wives were grieved and sorrowful and overwhelmed
with anguish of mind, and some let fly their hair and cried
aloud, and stretched out their arms and cried aloud, and
fell headlong to the ground and rolled to and fro, saying,
"All too soon will The Blessed One pass into Nirvana; all
too soon will The Happy One pass into Nirvana; all too
soon will The Light of the World vanish from sight." Then
the Mallas and their children and their daughters-in-law
and their wives, being grieved and sorrowful and overwhelmed with anguish of mind, drew near to the sal-tree
grove Upavattana of the Mallas, and to where the venerable
Ananda was.

Then it occurred to the venerable Ananda as follows:—

"If I shall cause the Kusinārā-Mallas one by one to do
reverence to The Blessed One, the day will dawn ere they
have finished. What if now I marshal the Mallas by families,
and cause them by families to do reverence to The Blessed
One, and say, 'Reverend Sir, a Malla named so-and-so, with
his children, his wife, his following, and his friends, bows
low in reverence at the feet of The Blessed One.'"

And the venerable Ananda marshalled the Mallas by
families, and caused them by families to do reverence to

The Blessed One, saying, "Reverend Sir, a Malla named so-and-so, with his children, his wife, his following, and his friends, bows low in reverence at the feet of The Blessed One." And the venerable Ananda by this device succeeded in causing all the Kusinārā-Mallas to do reverence to The Blessed One before the end of the first watch of the night.

Now at that time Subhadda, a wandering ascetic, was dwelling at Kusinārā. And Subhadda, the wandering ascetic, heard the report:—

"To-night, in the last watch, the monk Gotama will pass into Nirvana."

Then it occurred to Subhadda, the wandering ascetic, as follows:—

"I have heard wandering ascetics, that were old men, advanced in years, teachers, and teachers' teachers, declare, 'But seldom, and on rare occasions, does a Tathāgata, a saint, and Supreme Buddha arise in the world.' And to-night in the last watch, the monk Gotama will pass into Nirvana. And a certain question has arisen in my mind, and I am persuaded of the monk Gotama that he can so teach me the Doctrine that I shall be relieved of this my doubt."

Then Subhadda, the wandering ascetic, drew near to the sal-tree grove Upavattana of the Mallas, and to where the venerable Ananda was, and having drawn near, he spoke to the venerable Ananda as follows:—

"Ananda, I have heard wandering ascetics, that were old men, advanced in years, teachers, and teachers' teachers, declare, 'But seldom, and on rare occasions, does a Tathāgata, a saint, and Supreme Buddha arise in the world.' And tonight, in the last watch, the monk Gotama will pass into Nirvana. And a certain doubt has arisen in my mind, and I am persuaded of the monk Gotama that he can so teach me the Doctrine that I shall be relieved of this my doubt. Let me, then, Ananda, have an opportunity of seeing the monk Gotama."

When Subhadda, the wandering ascetic, had so spoken, the venerable Ananda spoke to him as follows:—

"Enough of that, brother Subhadda; trouble not The Tathāgata. The Blessed One is weary."

And a second time Subhadda, the wandering ascetic, . . .

And a third time Subhadda, the wandering ascetic, spoke to the venerable Ananda as follows:—

"Ananda, I have heard wandering ascetics, old men, advanced in years, teachers, and teachers' teachers, when they said, 'But seldom, and on rare occasions, does a Tathāgata, a saint, and Supreme Buddha arise in the world.' And to-night, in the last watch, the monk Gotama will pass into Nirvana. And a certain doubt has arisen in my mind, and I am persuaded of the monk Gotama that he can so teach me the Doctrine that I shall be relieved of this my doubt. Let me, then, Ananda, have an opportunity of seeing the monk Gotama."

And a third time the venerable Ananda spoke to Subhadda, the wandering ascetic, as follows:—

"Enough of that, brother Subhadda; trouble not The Tathāgata. The Blessed One is weary."

Now The Blessed One chanced to hear the conversation between the venerable Ananda and the wandering ascetic Subhadda. And The Blessed One called to the venerable Ananda:—

"Enough, Ananda; hinder not Subhadda. Let Subhadda, Amanda, have an opportunity of beholding The Tathāgata. Whatever Subhadda shall ask of me, he will ask for the sake of information, and not for the sake of troubling me, and he will quickly understand my answers to his questions."

Then the venerable Ananda spoke to Subhadda, the wandering ascetic, as follows:—

"You may come, brother Subhadda; The Blessed One grants you an audience."

Then Subhadda, the wandering ascetic, drew near to where The Blessed One was; and having drawn near, he exchanged greetings with The Blessed One; and having passed with him the greetings of friendship and civility, he sat down respectfully at one side. And seated respectfully at one side, Subhadda, the wandering ascetic, spoke to The Blessed One as follows:—

"Gotama, all those monks and Brahmans who possess a large following and crowds of hearers and disciples, and who are distinguished, renowned leaders of sects, and highly esteemed by the multitudes,—to wit, Pūrana Kassapa, Makkhali Gosāla, Ajita Kesakambali, Pakudha Kaccāyana, Sañjaya Belatthiputta, Nigantha Nāthaputta,—have they all done as they maintain, discovered the truth, or have they not? or have some of them done so, and others not?"

"Enough, O Subhadda, let us leave the question, 'Have they all done as they maintain, discovered the truth, or have they not? or have some of them done so, and others not?' The Doctrine will I teach you, Subhadda. Listen to me, and pay strict attention, and I will speak."

"Yes, Reverend Sir," said Subhadda, the wandering ascetic, to The Blessed One in assent. And The Blessed One spoke as follows:—

"Subhadda, in whatever doctrine and discipline the noble eightfold path is not found, therein also is not found the monk of the first degree, nor the monk of the second degree, nor the monk of the third degree, nor the monk of the fourth degree; and in whatever doctrine and discipline, O Subhadda, the noble eightfold path is found, therein also are found the monk of the first degree, and the monk of the second degree, and the monk of the third degree, and the monk of the fourth degree. Now in this Doctrine and Discipline, O Subhadda, the noble eightfold path is found: and therein alone, O Subhadda, are found the monk of the first degree, and the monk of the second degree, and the monk of the third degree, and the monk of the fourth degree. Destitute of true monks are all other creeds. But let these my priests, O Subhadda, live rightly, and the world will not be destitute of saints.

> "What time my age was twenty-nine, Subhadda,
> I left the world to seek the summum bonum.
> Now fifty years and more have passed, Subhadda,
> Since I renounced the world and lived ascetic
> Within the Doctrine's pale, that rule of conduct
> Outside of which no genuine monk existeth,

nor the monk of the second degree, nor the monk of the third degree, nor the monk of the fourth degree. Destitute of monks are all other creeds. But let these my priests, O Subhadda, live rightly, and the world will not be destitute of saints."

When The Blessed One had thus spoken, Subhadda, the wandering ascetic, spoke to him as follows:—

"O wonderful is it, Reverend Sir! O wonderful is it, Reverend Sir! It is as if, Reverend Sir, one were to set up that which was overturned, or were to disclose that which was hidden, or were to point out the way to a lost traveller, or were to carry a lamp into a dark place that they who had eyes might see forms. Even so has The Blessed One expounded the Doctrine in many different ways. Reverend Sir, I betake myself to The Blessed One for refuge, to the Doctrine, and to the Congregation of the priests. Suffer me to retire from the world under The Blessed One; suffer me to receive ordination."

"Subhadda, any one who aforetime has been an adherent of another sect and afterwards desires to retire from the world and receive ordination under this Doctrine and Discipline, must first spend four months on probation, and after the lapse of four months, strenuous-minded priests receive him into the Order and confer on him the priestly ordination. Nevertheless, in this matter of probation I recognize a difference in persons."

"Reverend Sir, if all they who aforetime have been adherents of other sects and afterwards desire to retire from the world and receive ordination under this Doctrine and Discipline, must first spend four months on probation, and after the lapse of four months strenuous-minded priests receive them into the Order, and confer on them the priestly ordination, then am I ready to spend four years on probation, and after the lapse of four years, let strenuous-minded priests receive me into the Order and confer on me the priestly ordination."

Then The Blessed One said to the venerable Ananda,

"Well, then, Ananda, receive Subhadda into the Order."

"Yes, Reverend Sir," said the venerable Ananda to The Blessed One in assent.

Then Subhadda, the wandering ascetic, spoke to the venerable Ananda as follows:—

"How fortunate you priests are, brother Ananda! How supremely fortunate, brother Ananda, that you all have been sprinkled with the sprinkling of discipleship at the hands of The Teacher himself."

And Subhadda, the wandering ascetic, retired from the world under The Blessed One, and received ordination. And without delay, after he had received ordination, the venerable Subhadda began to live solitary and retired, vigilant, strenuous, and zealous; and in no long time, and while yet alive, he came to learn for himself, and to realize, and to live in the possession of that highest good to which the holy life conducts, and for the sake of which youths of good family so nobly retire from the household life to the houseless one. And he knew that for him rebirth was exhausted, that he had lived the holy life, that he had done what it behooved him to do, and that he was no more for this world. So the venerable Subhadda became of the number of the saints, and he was the last disciple made by The Blessed One himself.

End of the Hiraññavati Recitation, which is the Fifth.

Then The Blessed One addressed the venerable Ananda:—

"It may be, Ananda, that some of you will think, 'The word of The Teacher is a thing of the past; we have now no Teacher.' But that, Ananda, is not the correct view. The Doctrine and Discipline, Ananda, which I have taught and enjoined upon you is to be your teacher when I am gone. But whereas now, Ananda, all the priests address each other with the title of 'brother,' not so must they address each other after I am gone. A senior priest, Ananda, is to address a junior priest either by his given name, or by his family name, or by the title of 'brother;' a junior priest is to address a senior priest with the title 'reverend sir,' or 'venerable.' If the Order, Ananda, wish to do so, after I am gone they may abrogate all the lesser and minor precepts. On Channa, Ananda, after I am gone, the higher penalty is to be inflicted."

"Reverend Sir, what is this higher penalty?"

"Let Channa, Ananda, say what he likes, he is not to be spoken to nor admonished nor instructed by the priests."

Then The Blessed One addressed the priests:—

"It may be, O priests, that some priest has a doubt or perplexity respecting either The Buddha or the Doctrine or the Order or the Path or the course of conduct. Ask any ques-

tions, O priests, and suffer not that afterwards ye feel remorse, saying, 'Our Teacher was present with us, but we
failed to ask him all our questions.' "

When he had so spoken, the priests remained silent.

And a second time The Blessed One, and a third time The
Blessed One addressed the priests:—

"It may be, O priests, that some priest has a doubt or perplexity respecting either The Buddha or the Doctrine or the
Order or the Path or the course of conduct. Ask any questions, O priests, and suffer not that afterwards ye feel remorse, saying, 'Our Teacher was present with us, but we
failed to ask him all our questions.' "

And a third time the priests remained silent.

Then The Blessed One addressed the priests:—

"It may be, O priests, that it is out of respect to The
Teacher that ye ask no questions. Then let each one speak to
his friend."

And when he had thus spoken, the priests remained silent. Then the venerable Ananda spoke to The Blessed One
as follows:—

"It is wonderful, Reverend Sir! It is marvellous, Reverend
Sir! Reverend Sir, I have faith to believe that in this congregation of priests not a single priest has a doubt or perplexity
respecting either The Buddha or the Doctrine or the Order
or the Path or the course of conduct."

"With you, Ananda, it is a matter of faith, when you say
that; but with the Tathāgata, Ananda, it is a matter of
knowledge that in this congregation of priests not a single
priest has a doubt or perplexity respecting either The Buddha or the Doctrine or the Order or the Path or the course of
conduct. For of all these five hundred priests, Ananda, the
most backward one has become converted, and is not liable
to pass into a lower state of existence, but is destined neces-
sarily to attain supreme wisdom."

Then The Blessed One addressed the priests:—

"And now, O priests, I take my leave of you; all the constituents of being are transitory; work out your salvation with diligence."

And this was the last word of The Tathāgata.

Thereupon The Blessed One entered the first trance; and rising from the first trance, he entered the second trance; and rising from the second trance, he entered the third trance; and rising from the third trance, he entered the fourth trance; and rising from the fourth trance, he entered the realm of the infinity of space; and rising from the realm of the infinity of space, he entered the realm of the infinity of consciousness; and rising from the realm of the infinity of consciousness, he entered the realm of nothingness; and rising from the realm of nothingness, he entered the realm of neither perception nor yet non-perception; and rising from the realm of neither perception nor yet non-perception, he arrived at the cessation of perception and sensation.

Thereupon the venerable Ananda spoke to the venerable Anuruddha as follows:—

"Reverend Anuruddha, The Blessed One has passed into Nirvana."

"Nay, brother Ananda, The Blessed One has not passed into Nirvana; he has arrived at the cessation of perception and sensation."

Thereupon The Blessed One rising from the cessation of his perception and sensation, entered the realm of neither perception nor yet non-perception; and rising from the realm of neither perception nor yet non-perception, he entered the realm of nothingness; and rising from the realm of nothingness, he entered the realm of the infinity of consciousness; and rising from the realm of the infinity of consciousness, he entered the realm of the infinity of space; and rising from the realm of the infinity of space, he entered the

fourth trance; and rising from the fourth trance, he entered
the third trance; and rising from the third trance, he entered
the second trance; and rising from the second trance, he entered the first trance; and rising from the first trance, he entered the second trance; and rising from the second trance,
he entered the third trance; and rising from the third trance,
he entered the fourth trance; and rising from the fourth
trance, immediately The Blessed One passed into Nirvana.

BUDDHIST WRITINGS
II. THE DOCTRINE

QUESTIONS WHICH TEND NOT TO EDIFICATION
Translated from the Majjhima-Nikāya, and
constituting Sutta 63

THUS have I heard.

On a certain occasion The Blessed One was dwelling at Sāvatthi in Jetavana monastery in Anāthapindika's Park. Now it happened to the venerable Māluṅkyāputta, being in seclusion and plunged in meditation, that a consideration presented itself to his mind, as follows:—

"These theories which The Blessed One has left unelucidated, has set aside and rejected,—that the world is eternal, that the world is not eternal, that the world is finite, that the world is infinite, that the soul and the body are identical, that the soul is one thing and the body another, that the saint exists after death, that the saint does not exist after death, that the saint both exists and does not exist after death, that the saint neither exists nor does not exist after death,—these The Blessed One does not elucidate to me. And the fact that The Blessed One does not elucidate them to me does not please me nor suit me. Therefore I will draw near to The Blessed One and inquire of him concerning this matter. If The Blessed One will elucidate to me, either that the world is eternal, or that the world is not eternal, or that the world is finite, or that the world is infinite, or that the soul and the body are identical, or that the soul is one thing and the body another, or that the saint exists after death, or that the saint does not exist after death, or that the saint both exists and

55

does not exist after death, or that the saint neither exists nor does not exist after death, in that case will I lead the religious life under The Blessed One. If The Blessed One will not elucidate to me, either that the world is eternal, or that the world is not eternal, . . . or that the saint neither exists nor does not exist after death, in that case will I abandon religious training and return to the lower life of a layman."

Then the venerable Māluṅkyāputta arose at eventide from his seclusion, and drew near to where The Blessed One was; and having drawn near and greeted The Blessed One, he sat down respectfully at one side. And seated respectfully at one side, the venerable Māluṅkyāputta spoke to The Blessed One as follows:—

"Reverend Sir, it happened to me, as I was just now in seclusion and plunged in meditation, that a consideration presented itself to my mind; as follows: 'These theories which The Blessed One has left unelucidated, has set aside and rejected,—that the world is eternal, that the world is not eternal, . . . that the saint neither exists nor does not exist after death,—these The Blessed One does not elucidate to me. And the fact that The Blessed One does not elucidate them to me does not please me nor suit me. I will draw near to The Blessed One and inquire of him concerning this matter. If The Blessed One will elucidate to me, either that the world is eternal, or that the world is not eternal, . . . or that the saint neither exists nor does not exist after death, in that case will I lead the religious life under The Blessed One. If The Blessed One will not elucidate to me, either that the world is eternal, or that the world is not eternal, . . . or that the saint neither exists nor does not exist after death, in that case will I abandon religious training and return to the lower life of a layman.'

"If The Blessed One knows that the world is eternal, let The Blessed One elucidate to me that the world is eternal; if

The Blessed One knows that the world is not eternal, let The Blessed One elucidate to me that the world is not eternal. If the Blessed One does not know either that the world is eternal or that the world is not eternal, the only upright thing for one who does not know, or who has not that insight, is to say, 'I do not know; I have not that insight.'

"If The Blessed One knows that the world is finite, . . . '

"If The Blessed One knows that the soul and the body are identical, . . . '

"If The Blessed One knows that the saint exists after death, . . . '

"If The Blessed One knows that the saint both exists and does not exist after death, let The Blessed One elucidate to me that the saint both exists and does not exist after death; if The Blessed One knows that the saint neither exists nor does not exist after death, let The Blessed One elucidate to me that the saint neither exists nor does not exist after death. If The Blessed One does not know either that the saint both exists and does not exist after death, or that the saint neither exists nor does not exist after death, the only upright thing for one who does not know, or who has not that insight, is to say, 'I do not know; I have not that insight.' "

"Pray, Māluṅkyāputta, did I ever say to you, 'Come, Māluṅkyāputta, lead the religious life under me, and I will elucidate to you either that the world is eternal, or that the world is not eternal, . . . or that the saint neither exists nor does not exist after death'?"

"Nay, verily, Reverend Sir."

"Or did you ever say to me, 'Reverend Sir, I will lead the religious life under The Blessed One, on condition that The Blessed One elucidate to me either that the world is eternal, or that the world is not eternal, . . . or that the saint neither exists nor does not exist after death'?"

"Nay, verily, Reverend Sir."

"So you acknowledged, Māluñkyāputta, that I have not said to you, 'Come, Māluñkyāputta, lead the religious life under me and I will elucidate to you either that the world is eternal, or that the world is not eternal, . . . or that the saint neither exists nor does not exist after death;' and again that you have not said to me, 'Reverend Sir, I will lead the religious life under The Blessed One, on condition that The Blessed One elucidate to me either that the world is eternal, or that the world is not eternal, . . . or that the saint neither exists nor does not exist after death.' That being the case, vain man, whom are you so angrily denouncing?

"Māluñkyāputta, any one who should say, 'I will not lead the religious life under The Blessed One until The Blessed One shall elucidate to me either that the world is eternal, or that the world is not eternal, . . . or that the saint neither exists nor does not exist after death;'—that person would die, Māluñkyāputta, before The Tathāgata had ever elucidated this to him.

"It is as if, Māluñkyāputta, a man had been wounded by an arrow thickly smeared with poison, and his friends and companions, his relatives and kinsfolk, were to procure for him a physician or surgeon; and the sick man were to say, 'I will not have this arrow taken out until I have learnt whether the man who wounded me belonged to the warrior caste, or to the Brahman caste, or to the agricultural caste, or to the menial caste.'

"Or again he were to say, 'I will not have this arrow taken out until I have learnt the name of the man who wounded me, and to what clan he belongs.'

"Or again he were to say, 'I will not have this arrow taken out until I have learnt whether the man who wounded me was tall, or short, or of the middle height.'

"Or again he were to say, 'I will not have this arrow taken

out until I have learnt whether the man who wounded me was black, or dusky, or of a yellow skin.'

"Or again he were to say, 'I will not have this arrow taken out until I have learnt whether the man who wounded me was from this or that village, or town, or city.'

"Or again he were to say, 'I will not have this arrow taken out until I have learnt whether the bow which wounded me was a cāpa, or a kodanda.'

"Or again he were to say, 'I will not have this arrow taken out until I have learnt whether the bow-string which wounded me was made from swallow-wort, or bamboo, or sinew, or maruva, or from milk-weed.'

"Or again he were to say, 'I will not have this arrow taken out until I have learnt whether the shaft which wounded me was a kaccha or a ropima.'

"Or again he were to say, 'I will not have this arrow taken out until I have learnt whether the shaft which wounded me was feathered from the wings of a vulture, or of a heron, or of a falcon, or of a peacock, or of a sithilahanu.

"Or again he were to say, 'I will not have this arrow taken out until I have learnt whether the shaft which wounded me was wound round with the sinews of an ox, or of a buffalo, or of a ruru deer, or of a monkey.'

"Or again he were to say, 'I will not have this arrow taken out until I have learnt whether the arrow which wounded me was an ordinary arrow, or a claw-headed arrow, or a vekanda, or an iron arrow, or a calf-tooth arrow, or a karavī-rapapatta.' That man would die, Māluṅkyāputta, without ever having learnt this. In exactly the same way, Māluṅky-āputta, any one who should say, 'I will not lead the religious life under The Blessed One until The Blessed One shall elucidate to me either that the world is eternal, or that the world is not eternal, ... or that the saint neither exists nor does not exist after death;'—that person would die,

Māluṅkyāputta, before The Tathāgata had ever elucidated this to him.

"The religious life, Māluṅkyāputta, does not depend on the dogma that the world is eternal; nor does the religious life, Māluṅkyāputta, depend on the dogma that the world is not eternal. Whether the dogma obtain, Māluṅkyāputta, that the world is eternal, or that the world is not eternal, there still remain birth, old age, death, sorrow, lamentation, misery, grief, and despair, for the extinction of which in the present life I am prescribing.

"The religious life, Māluṅkyāputta, does not depend on the dogma that the world is finite; . . .

"The religious life, Māluṅkyāputta, does not depend on the dogma that the soul and the body are identical; . . .

"The religious life, Māluṅkyāputta, does not depend on the dogma that the saint exists after death; . . .

"The religious life, Māluṅkyāputta, does not depend on the dogma that the saint both exists and does not exist after death; nor does the religious life, Māluṅkyāputta, depend on the dogma that the saint neither exists nor does not exist after death. Whether the dogma obtain, Māluṅkyāputta, that the saint both exists and does not exist after death, or that the saint neither exists nor does not exist after death, there still remain birth, old age, death, sorrow, lamentation, misery, grief, and despair, for the extinction of which in the present life I am prescribing.

"Accordingly, Māluṅkyāputta, bear always in mind what it is that I have not elucidated, and what it is that I have elucidated. And what, Māluṅkyāputta, have I not elucidated? I have not elucidated, Māluṅkyāputta, that the world is eternal; I have not elucidated that the world is not eternal; I have not elucidated that the world is finite; I have not elucidated that the world is infinite; I have not elucidated that the soul and the body are identical; I have not elucidated that the soul is one thing and the body another; I have not elucidated that the saint exists after death; I have not elucidated that the saint does not exist after death; I have not elucidated that the saint both exists and does not exist after death; I have not elucidated that the saint neither exists nor does not exist after death. And why, Māluṅkyāputta, have I not elucidated this? Because, Māluṅkyāputta, this profits not, nor has to do with the fundamentals of religion, nor tends to aversion, absence of passion, cessation, quiescence, the supernatural faculties, supreme wisdom, and Nirvana; therefore have I not elucidated it.

"And what, Māluṅkyāputta, have I elucidated? Misery, Māluṅkyāputta, have I elucidated; the origin of misery have I elucidated; the cessation of misery have I elucidated; and the path leading to the cessation of misery have I elucidated. And why, Māluṅkyāputta, have I elucidated this? Because, Māluṅkyāputta, this does profit; has to do with the fundamentals of religion, and tends to aversion, absence of passion, cessation, quiescence, knowledge, supreme wisdom, and Nirvana; therefore have I elucidated it. Accordingly, Māluṅkyāputta, bear always in mind what it is that I have not elucidated, and what it is that I have elucidated."

Thus spake The Blessed One; and, delighted, the venerable Māluṅkyāputta applauded the speech of The Blessed One.

The Lesser Māluṅkyāputta Sermon.

THERE IS NO EGO

1. Translated from the Milindapañha (25[1])

THEN drew near Milinda the king to where the venerable
Nāgasena was; and having drawn near he greeted the venerable Nāgasena; and having passed the compliments of
friendship and civility, he sat down respectfully at one side.
And the venerable Nāgasena returned the greeting; by which,
verily, he won the heart of king Milinda.

And Milinda the king spoke to the venerable Nāgasena
as follows:—

"How is your reverence called? Bhante, what is your
name?"

"Your majesty, I am called Nāgasena; my fellow-priests,
your majesty, address me as Nāgasena: but whether parents
give one the name Nāgasena, or Sūrasena, or Vīrasena, or
Sīhasena, it is, nevertheless, your majesty, but a way of
counting, a term, an appellation, a convenient designation,
a mere name, this Nāgasena; for there is no Ego here to be
found."

Then said Milinda the king,—

"Listen to me, my lords, ye five hundred Yonakas, and ye
eighty thousand priests! Nāgasena here says thus: 'There is
no Ego here to be found.' Is it possible, pray, for me to assent to what he says?"

And Milinda the king spoke to the venerable Nāgasena
as follows:—

"Bhante Nāgasena, if there is no Ego to be found, who is

it then furnishes you priests with the priestly requisites,—robes, food, bedding, and medicine, the reliance of the sick? who is it makes use of the same? who is it keeps the precepts? who is it applies himself to meditation? who is it realizes the Paths, the Fruits, and Nirvana? who is it destroys life? who is it takes what is not given him? who is it commits immorality? who is it tells lies? who is it drinks intoxicating liquor? who is it commits the five crimes that constitute 'proximate karma?'[1] In that case, there is no merit; there is no demerit; there is no one who does or causes to be done meritorious or demeritorious deeds; neither good nor evil deeds can have any fruit or result. Bhante Nāgasena, neither is he a murderer who kills a priest, nor can you priests, bhante Nāgasena, have any teacher, preceptor, or ordination. When you say, 'My fellow-priests, your majesty, address me as Nāgasena,' what then is this Nāgasena? Pray, bhante, is the hair of the head Nāgasena?"

"Nay, verily, your majesty."

"Is the hair of the body Nāgasena?"

"Nay, verily, your majesty."

"Are nails . . . teeth . . . skin . . . flesh . . . sinews . . . bones . . . marrow of the bones . . . kidneys . . . heart . . . liver . . . pleura . . . spleen . . . lungs . . . intestines . . . mesentery . . . stomach . . . faeces . . . bile . . . phlegm . . . pus . . . blood . . .

---

[1]Translated from the Sārasaṅgaha, as quoted in Trenckner's note to this passage:

"By *proximate karma* is meant karma that ripens in the next existence. To show what this is, I [the author of the Sārasaṅgaha] give the following passage from the Atthānasutta of the first book of the Aṅguttara-Nikāya:—'It is an impossibility, O priests, the case can never occur, that an individual imbued with the correct doctrine should deprive his mother of life, should deprive his father of life, should deprive a saint of life, should in a revengeful spirit cause a bloody wound to a Tathāgata, should cause a schism in the church. This is an impossibility.' "

sweat . . . fat . . . tears . . . lymph . . . saliva . . . snot . . . syn-ovial fluid . . . urine . . . brain of the head Nāgasena?"

"Nay, verily, your majesty."

"Is now, bhante, form Nāgasena?"

"Nay, verily, your majesty."

"Is sensation Nāgasena?"

"Nay, verily, your majesty."

"Is perception Nāgasena?"

"Nay, verily, your majesty."

"Are the predispositions Nāgasena?"

"Nay, verily, your majesty."

"Is consciousness Nāgasena?"

"Nay, verily, your majesty."

"Are, then, bhante, form, sensation, perception, the pre-dispositions, and consciousness unitedly Nāgasena?"

"Nay, verily, your majesty."

"Is it, then, bhante, something besides form, sensation, perception, the predispositions, and consciousness, which is Nāgasena?"

"Nay, verily, your majesty."

"Bhante, although I question you very closely, I fail to discover any Nāgasena. Verily, now, bhante, Nāgasena is a mere empty sound. What Nāgasena is there here? Bhante, you speak a falsehood, a lie: there is no Nāgasena."

Then the venerable Nāgasena spoke to Milinda the king as follows:—

"Your majesty, you are a delicate prince, an exceedingly delicate prince; and if, your majesty, you walk in the middle of the day on hot sandy ground, and you tread on rough grit, gravel, and sand, your feet become sore, your body tired, the mind is oppressed, and the body-consciousness suffers. Pray, did you come afoot, or riding?"

"Bhante, I do not go afoot: I came in a chariot."

"Your majesty, if you came in a chariot, declare to me the chariot. Pray, your majesty, is the pole the chariot?"

"Nay, verily, bhante."

"Is the axle the chariot?"

"Nay, verily, bhante."

"Are the wheels the chariot?"

"Nay, verily, bhante."

"Is the chariot-body the chariot?"

"Nay, verily, bhante."

"Is the banner-staff the chariot?"

"Nay, verily, bhante."

"Is the yoke the chariot?"

"Nay, verily, bhante."

"Are the reins the chariot?"

"Nay, verily, bhante."

"Is the goading-stick the chariot?"

"Nay, verily, bhante."

"Pray, your majesty, are pole, axle, wheels, chariot-body, banner-staff, yoke, reins, and goad unitedly the chariot?"

"Nay, verily, bhante."

"Is it, then, your majesty, something else besides pole, axle, wheels, chariot-body, banner-staff, yoke, reins and goad which is the chariot?"

"Nay, verily, bhante."

"Your majesty, although I question you very closely, I fail to discover any chariot. Verily now, your majesty, the word chariot is a mere empty sound. What chariot is there here? Your majesty, you speak a falsehood, a lie: there is no chariot. Your majesty, you are the chief king in all the continent of India; of whom are you afraid that you speak a lie? Listen to me, my lords, ye five hundred Yonakas, and ye eighty thousand priests! Milinda the king here says thus: 'I came in a chariot;' and being requested, 'Your majesty, if you came in a chariot, declare to me the chariot,' he fails to produce any chariot. Is it possible, pray, for me to assent to what he says?"

When he had thus spoken, the five hundred Yonakas applauded the venerable Nāgasena and spoke to Milinda the king as follows:—

"Now, your majesty, answer, if you can."

Then Milinda the king spoke to the venerable Nāgasena as follows:—

"Bhante Nāgasena, I speak no lie: the word 'chariot' is but a way of counting, term, appellation, convenient designation, and name for pole, axle, wheels, chariot-body, and banner-staff."

"Thoroughly well, your majesty, do you understand a chariot. In exactly the same way, your majesty, in respect of me, Nāgasena is but a way of counting, term, appellation, convenient designation, mere name for the hair of my head, hair of my body . . . brain of the head, form, sensation, perception, the predispositions, and consciousness. But in the absolute sense there is no Ego here to be found. And the priestess Vajirā, your majesty, said as follows in the presence of The Blessed One:—

> " 'Even as the word of "chariot" means
> That members join to frame a whole;
> So when the Groups appear to view,
> We use the phrase, "A living being.[2]" ' "

"It is wonderful, bhante Nāgasena! It is marvellous, bhante Nāgasena! Brilliant and prompt is the wit of your replies. If The Buddha were alive, he would applaud. Well

[2] That is, "a living entity."

done, well done, Nāgasena! Brilliant and prompt is the wit of your replies."

2. Translated from the Visuddhi-Magga (chap. xviii)

Just as the word "chariot" is but a mode of expression for axle, wheels, chariot-body, pole, and other constituent members, placed in a certain relation to each other, but when we come to examine the members one by one, we discover that in the absolute sense there is no chariot; and just as the word "house" is but a mode of expression for wood and other constituents of a house, surrounding space in a certain relation, but in the absolute sense there is no house; and just as the word "fist" is but a mode of expression for the fingers, the thumb, etc., in a certain relation; and the word "lute" for the body of the lute, strings, etc.; "army" for elephants, horses, etc.; "city" for fortifications, houses, gates, etc.; "tree" for trunk, branches, foliage, etc., in a certain relation, but when we come to examine the parts one by one, we discover that in the absolute sense there is no tree; in exactly the same way the words "living entity" and "Ego," are but a mode of expression for the presence of the five attachment groups, but when we come to examine the elements of being one by one, we discover that in the absolute sense there is no living entity there to form a basis for such figments as "I am," or "I"; in other words, that in the absolute sense there is only name and form. The insight of him who perceives this is called knowledge of the truth.

He, however, who abandons this knowledge of the truth and believes in a living entity must assume either that this living entity will perish or that it will not perish. If he assume that it will not perish, he falls into the heresy of the persistence of existences; or if he assume that it will perish, he falls into that of the annihilation of existences. And why do I say so? Because, just as sour cream has milk as its antecedent, so nothing here exists but what has its own antecedents. To say, "The living entity persists," is to fall short of the truth; to say, "It is annihilated," is to outrun the truth. Therefore has The Blessed One said:—

"There are two heresies, O priests, which possess both gods and men, by which some fall short of the truth, and some outrun the truth; but the intelligent know the truth.

"And how, O priests, do some fall short of the truth?

"O priests, gods and men delight in existence, take pleasure in existence, rejoice in existence, so that when the Doctrine for the cessation of existence is preached to them, their minds do not leap toward it, are not favorably disposed toward it, do not rest in it, do not adopt it.

"Thus, O priests, do some fall short of the truth."

"And how, O priests, do some outrun the truth?

"Some are distressed at, ashamed of, and loathe existence, and welcome the thought of non-existence, saying, 'See here! When they say that on the dissolution of the body this Ego is annihilated, perishes, and does not exist after death, that is good, that is excellent, that is as it should be.'

"Thus, O priests, do some outrun the truth.

"And how, O priests, do the intelligent know the truth?

"We may have, O priests, a priest who knows things as they really are, and knowing things as they really are, he is on the road to aversion for things, to absence of passion for them, and to cessation from them.

"Thus, O priests, do the intelligent know the truth."

3.—Translated from the Mahā-Nidāna-Sutta (256[21]) of the Dīgha-Nikāya

"In regard to the Ego, Ananda, what are the views held concerning it?

"In regard to the Ego, Ananda, either one holds the view that sensation is the Ego, saying, 'Sensation is my Ego;'

"Or, in regard to the Ego, Ananda, one holds the view, 'Verily, sensation is not my Ego; my Ego has no sensation;'

"Or, in regard to the Ego, Ananda, one holds the view, 'Verily, neither is sensation my Ego, nor does my Ego have no sensation. My Ego has sensation; my Ego possesses the faculty of sensation.'

"In the above case, Ananda, where it is said, 'Sensation is my Ego,' reply should be made as follows: 'Brother, there are three sensations: the pleasant sensation, the unpleasant sensation, and the indifferent sensation. Which of these three sensations do you hold to be the Ego?'

"Whenever, Ananda, a person experiences a pleasant sensation, he does not at the same time experience an unpleasant sensation, nor does he experience an indifferent sensation; only the pleasant sensation does he then feel. Whenever, Ananda, a person experiences an unpleasant sensation, he does not at the same time experience a pleasant sensation, nor does he experience an indifferent sensation; only the unpleasant sensation does he then feel. Whenever, Ananda, a person experiences an indifferent sensation, he does not at the same time experience a pleasant sensation, nor does he experience an unpleasant sensation; only the indifferent sensation does he then feel.

"Now pleasant sensations, Ananda, are transitory, are due to causes, originate by dependence, and are subject to decay, disappearance, effacement, and cessation; and unpleasant sensations, Ananda, are transitory, are due to causes, originate by dependence, and are subject to decay, disappearance, effacement, and cessation; and indifferent sensations, Ananda, are transitory, are due to causes, originate by dependence, and are subject to decay, disappearance, effacement, and cessation. While this person is experiencing a pleasant sensation, he thinks, 'This is my Ego.' And after the cessation of this same pleasant sensation, he thinks, 'My Ego has passed away.' While he is experiencing an unpleasant sensation, he thinks, 'This is my Ego.' And after the cessation of this same unpleasant sensation, he thinks, 'My Ego has passed away.' And while he is experiencing an indifferent sensation, he thinks, 'This is my Ego.' And after the cessation of this same indifferent sensation, he thinks, 'My Ego has passed away.' So that he who says, 'Sensation is my Ego,' holds the view that even during his lifetime his Ego is transitory, that it is pleasant, unpleasant, or mixed, and that it is subject to rise and disappearance.

" Accordingly, Ananda, it is not possible to hold the view, 'Sensation is my Ego.'

"In the above case, Ananda, where it is said, 'Verily, sensation is not my Ego; my Ego has no sensation,' reply should be made as follows: 'But, brother, where there is no sensation, is there any "I am"?' "

"Nay, verily, Reverend Sir."

"Accordingly, Ananda, it is not possible to hold the view, 'Verily, sensation is not my Ego; my Ego has no sensation.'

"In the above case, Ananda, where it is said, 'Verily, neither is sensation my Ego, nor does my Ego have no sensation. My Ego has sensation; my Ego possesses the faculty of sensation,' reply should be made as follows: 'Suppose, brother, that utterly and completely, and without remainder, all sensation were to cease—if there were nowhere any sensation, pray, would there be anything, after the cessation of sensation, of which it could be said, "This am I"?'"

"Nay, verily, Reverend Sir."

"Accordingly, Ananda, it is not possible to hold the view, 'Verily, neither is sensation my Ego, nor does my Ego have no sensation. My Ego has sensation; my Ego possesses the faculty of sensation.'

"From the time Ananda, a priest no longer holds the view that sensation is the Ego, no longer holds the view that the Ego has no sensation, no longer holds the view that the Ego has sensation, possesses the faculty of sensation, he ceases to attach himself to anything in the world, and being free from attachment, he is never agitated, and being never agitated, he attains to Nirvana in his own person; and he knows that rebirth is exhausted, that he has lived the holy life, that he has done what it behooved him to do, and that he is no more for this world.

"Now it is impossible, Ananda, that to a mind so freed a priest should attribute the heresy that the saint exists after death, or that the saint does not exist after death, or that the saint both exists and does not exist after death, or that the saint neither exists nor does not exist after death.

"And why do I say so?

"Because, Ananda, after a priest has been freed by a thorough comprehension of affirmation and affirmation's range, of predication and predication's range, of declaration and declaration's range, of knowledge and knowledge's field of action, of rebirth and what rebirth affects, it is impossible for him to attribute such a heretical lack of knowledge and perception to a priest similarly freed."

THE MIDDLE DOCTRINE

1.—Translated from the Samyutta-Nikāya (xxii. 90[16])

THE world, for the most part, O Kaccāna, holds either to a belief in being or to a belief in non-being. But for one who in the light of the highest knowledge, O Kaccāna, considers how the world arises, belief in the non-being of the world passes away. And for one who in the light of the highest knowledge, O Kaccāna, considers how the world ceases, belief in the being of the world passes away. The world, O Kaccāna, is for the most part bound up in a seeking, attachment, and proclivity [for the groups], but a priest does not sympathize with this seeking and attachment, nor with the mental affirmation, proclivity, and prejudice which affirms an Ego. He does not doubt or question that it is only evil that springs into existence, and only evil that ceases from existence, and his conviction of this fact is dependent on no one besides himself. This, O Kaccāna, is what constitutes Right Belief.

That things have being, O Kaccāna, constitutes one extreme of doctrine; that things have no being is the other extreme. These extremes, O Kaccāna, have been avoided by The Tathāgata, and it is a middle doctrine he teaches:—

On ignorance depends karma;
On karma depends consciousness;
On consciousness depend name and form;
On name and form depend the six organs of sense;
On the six organs of sense depends contact;

On contact depends sensation;
On sensation depends desire;
On desire depends attachment;
On attachment depends existence;
On existence depends birth;
On birth depend old age and death, sorrow, lamentation, misery, grief, and despair. Thus does this entire aggregation of misery arise.

But on the complete fading out and cessation of ignorance ceases Karma;

On the cessation of karma ceases consciousness;
On the cessation of consciousness cease name and form;
On the cessation of name and form cease the six organs of sense;
On the cessation of the six organs of sense ceases contact;
On the cessation of contact ceases sensation;
On the cessation of sensation ceases desire;
On the cessation of desire ceases attachment;
On the cessation of attachment ceases existence;
On the cessation of existence ceases birth;
On the cessation of birth cease old age and death, sorrow, lamentation, misery, grief, and despair. Thus does this entire aggregation of misery cease.

2.—Translated from the Samyutta-Nikāya (xii. 35[1])

Thus have I heard.
On a certain occasion The Blessed One was dwelling at Sāvatthi in Jetavana monastery in Anāthapindika's Park. And there The Blessed One addressed the priests.
"Priests," said he.

"Lord," said the priests to The Blessed One in reply.

And The Blessed One spoke as follows:

"O priests, on ignorance depends karma; . . . Thus does this entire aggregation of misery arise."

"Reverend Sir, what are old age and death? and what is it has old age and death?"

"The question is not rightly put," said The Blessed One. "O priest to say: 'What are old age and death? and what is it has old age and death?' and to say: 'Old age and death are one thing, but it is another thing which has old age and death,' is to say the same thing in different ways. If, O priest, the dogma obtain that the soul and the body are identical, then there is no religious life; or if, O priest, the dogma obtain that the soul is one thing and the body another, then also there is no religious life. Both these extremes, O priest, have been avoided by The Tathāgata, and it is a middle doctrine he teaches: 'On birth depend old age and death.'"

"Reverend Sir, what is birth? and what is it has birth?"

"The question is not rightly put," said The Blessed One. "O priest, to say: 'What is birth? and what is it has birth?' and to say: 'Birth is one thing, but it is another thing which has birth,' is to say the same thing in different ways. If, O priest, the dogma obtain that the soul and the body are identical, then there is no religious life; or if, O priest, the dogma obtain that the soul is one thing and the body another, then also there is no religious life. Both these extremes, O priest, have been avoided by The Tathāgata, and it is a middle doctrine he teaches: 'On existence depends birth.'"

"Reverend Sir, what is existence? . . . attachment? . . . desire? . . . sensation? . . . contact? . . . the six organs of sense? . . . name and form? . . . consciousness? . . . karma? and what is it has karma?"

"The question is not rightly put," said The Blessed One. "O priest, to say: 'What is karma? and what is it has karma?' and to say: 'Karma is one thing, but it is another thing which has karma,' is to say the same thing in different ways. If, O priest, the dogma obtain that the soul and the body are identical, then there is no religious life; or if, O priest, the dogma obtain that the soul is one thing and the body another, then also there is no religious life. Both these extremes, O priest, have been avoided by The Tathāgata, and it is a middle doctrine he teaches: 'On ignorance depends karma.'

"But on the complete fading out and cessation of ignorance, O priest, all these refuges, puppet-shows, resorts, and writhings,—to wit: What are old age and death? and what is it has old age and death? or, old age and death are one thing, but it is another thing which has old age and death; or, the soul and the body are identical, or the soul is one thing, and the body another,—all such refuges of whatever kind are abandoned, uprooted, pulled out of the ground like a palmyra-tree, and become non-existent and not liable to spring up again in the future.

"But on the complete fading out and cessation of ignorance, O priest, all these refuges, puppet-shows, resorts, and writhings,—to wit: What is birth? . . . existence? attachment? . . . desire? . . . sensation? . . . contact? . . . the six organs of sense? . . . name and form? . . . consciousness? . . . karma? and what is it has karma? or, karma is one thing, but it is another thing which has karma; or, the soul and the body are identical, or the soul is one thing and the body another,—all such refuges are abandoned, uprooted, pulled out of the ground like a palmyra-tree, and become non-existent and not liable to spring up again in the future."

3.—Translated from the Visuddhi-Magga (chap. xvii.)

Inasmuch as it is dependently on each other and in unison and simultaneously that the factors which constitute dependence originate the elements of being, therefore did The Sage call these factors Dependent Origination.

For the ignorance etc. which have been enumerated as constituting dependence, when they originate any of the elements of being, namely, karma and the rest, can only do so when dependent on each other and in case none of their number is lacking. Therefore it is dependently on each other and in unison and simultaneously that the factors which constitute dependence originate the elements of being, not by a part of their number nor by one succeeding the other. Accordingly The Sage, skilful in the art of discovering the signification of things, calls this dependence by the name of Dependent Origination.

And in so doing by the first of these two words is shown the falsity of such heresies as that of the persistence of existences, and by the second word, a rejection of such heresies as that existences cease to be, while by both together is shown the truth.

By the first:—The word "Dependent," as exhibiting a full complement of dependence and inasmuch as the elements of being are subject to that full complement of dependence, shows an avoidance of such heresies as that of the persistence of existences, the heresies, namely, of the persistence of existences, of uncaused existences, of existences due to an overruling power, of self-determining existences. For what have persistent existences, uncaused existences, etc., to do with a full complement of dependence?

By the second word:—The word "Origination," as exhibiting an origination of the elements of being and inasmuch as the elements of being originate by means of a full comple-

ment of dependence, shows a rejection of such heresies as
that of the annihilation of existences, the heresies, namely,
of the annihilation of existences, of nihilism, of the ineffi-
cacy of karma. For if the elements of being are continually
originating by means of an antecedent dependence, whence
can we have annihilation of existence, nihilism, and an inef-
ficacy of karma?

By both together:—By the complete phrase "Dependent
Origination," inasmuch as such and such elements of being
come into existence by means of an unbroken series of their
full complement of dependence, the truth, or middle course,
is shown. This rejects the heresy that he who experiences
the fruit of the deed is the same as the one who performed
the deed, and also rejects the converse one that he who experiences the fruit of a deed is different from the one who
performed the deed, and leaning not to either of these popular hypotheses, holds fast by nominalism.

KARMA

Translated from the Visuddhi-Magga (chap. xvii.)

THE kinds of karma are those already briefly mentioned, as consisting of the triplet beginning with meritorious karma and the triplet beginning with bodily karma, making six in all.

To give them here in full, however, meritorious karma consists of the eight meritorious thoughts which belong to the realm of sensual pleasure and show themselves in almsgiving, keeping the precepts, etc., and of the five meritorious thoughts which belong to the realm of form and show themselves in ecstatic meditation,—making thirteen thoughts; demeritorious karma consists of the twelve demeritorious thoughts which show themselves in the taking of life, etc.; and karma leading to immovability consists of the four meritorious thoughts which belong to the realm of formlessness and show themselves in ecstatic meditation. Accordingly these three karmas consist of twenty-nine thoughts.

As regards the other three, bodily karma consists of the thoughts of the body, vocal karma of the thoughts of the voice, mental karma of the thoughts of the mind. The object of this triplet is to show the avenues by which meritorious karma, etc., show themselves at the moment of the initiation of karma.

For bodily karma consists of an even score of thoughts, namely, of the eight meritorious thoughts which belong to the realm of sensual pleasure and of the twelve demeritorious ones. These by exciting gestures show themselves through the avenue of the body.

Vocal karma is when these same thoughts by exciting speech show themselves through the avenue of the voice. The thoughts, however, which belong to the realm of form, are not included, as they do not form a dependence for subsequent consciousness. And the case is the same with the thoughts which belong to the realm of formlessness. Therefore they also are to be excluded from the dependence of consciousness. However, all depend on ignorance.

Mental karma, however, consists of all the twenty-nine thoughts, when they spring up in the mind without exciting either gesture or speech.

Thus, when it is said that ignorance is the dependence of the karma-triplet consisting of meritorious karma, etc., it is to be understood that the other triplet is also included.

But it may be asked, "How can we tell that these karmas are dependent on ignorance?" Because they exist when ignorance exists.

For, when a person has not abandoned the want of knowledge concerning misery, etc., which is called ignorance, then by that want of knowledge concerning misery and concerning anteriority, etc., he seizes on the misery of the round of rebirth with the idea that it is happiness and hence begins to perform the threefold karma which is its cause; by that want of knowledge concerning the origin of misery and by being under the impression that thus happiness is secured, he begins to perform karma that ministers to desire, though such karma is really the cause of misery; and by that want of knowledge concerning cessation and the path and under the impression that some particular form of existence will prove to be the cessation of misery, although it really is not so, or that sacrifices, alarming the gods by the greatness of his austerities, and other like procedures are the way to cessation, although they are not such a way, he begins to perform the threefold karma.

Moreover, through this non-abandonment of ignorance in respect of the Four Truths, he does not know the fruition of meritorious karma to be the misery it really is, seeing that it is completely overwhelmed with the calamities, birth, old age, disease, death, etc.; and so to obtain it he begins to perform meritorious karma in its three divisions of bodily, vocal, and mental karma, just as a man in love with a heavenly nymph will throw himself down a precipice. When he does not perceive that at the end of that meritorious fruition considered to be such happiness comes the agonizing misery of change and disappointment, he begins to perform the meritorious karma above described, just as a locust will fly into the flame of a lamp, or a man that is greedy after honey will lick the honey-smeared edge of a knife. When he fails to perceive the calamities due to sensual gratification and its fruition, and, being under the impression that sensuality is happiness, lives enthralled by his passions, he then begins to perform demeritorious karma through the three avenues, just as a child will play with filth, or one who wishes to die will eat poison. When he does not perceive the misery of the change that takes place in the constituents of being, even in the realm of formlessness, but has a perverse belief in persistence, etc., he begins to perform mental karma that leads to immovability, just as a man who has lost his way will go after a mirage.

As, therefore, karma exists when ignorance exists but not when it does not exist, it is to be understood that this karma depends on ignorance. And it has been said as follows:

"O priests, the ignorant, uninstructed man performs meritorious karma, demeritorious karma, and karma leading to immovability. But whenever, O priests, he abandons his ignorance and acquires wisdom, he through the fading out of ignorance and the coming into being of wisdom does not even perform meritorious karma."

FRUITFUL AND BARREN KARMA

1.—Translated from the Aṅguttara-Nikāya (iii. 33[1])

[I. FRUITFUL KARMA]

THERE are three conditions, O priests, under which deeds are produced. And what are the three? Covetousness is a condition under which deeds are produced; hatred is a condition under which deeds are produced; infatuation is a condition under which deeds are produced.

When a man's deeds, O priests, are performed through covetousness, arise from covetousness, are occasioned by covetousness, originate in covetousness, wherever his personality may be, there those deeds ripen, and wherever they ripen, there he experiences the fruition of those deeds, be it in the present life, or in some subsequent one.

When a man's deeds, O priests, are performed through hatred, . . . are performed through infatuation, arise from infatuation, are occasioned by infatuation, originate in infatuation, wherever his personality may be, there those deeds ripen, and wherever they ripen, there he experiences the fruition of those deeds, be it in the present life, or in some subsequent one.

It is like seed, O priests, that is uninjured, undecayed, unharmed by wind or heat, and is sound, and advantageously sown in a fertile field on well-prepared soil; if then rain falls in due season, then, O priests, will that seed attain to growth, increase, and development. In exactly the same way, O priests, when a man's deeds are performed through covetousness, arise from covetousness, are occasioned by covetousness, originate in covetousness, wherever his personality may be, there those deeds ripen, and wherever they ripen, there he experiences the fruition of those deeds, be it in the present life, or in some subsequent one; when a man's deeds are performed through hatred, . . . are performed through infatuation, arise from infatuation, are occasioned by infatuation, originate in infatuation, wherever his personality may be, there those deeds ripen, and wherever they ripen, there he experiences the fruition of those deeds, be it in the present life, or in some subsequent one.

These, O priests, are the three conditions under which deeds are produced.

[II. Barren Karma]

There are three conditions, O priests, under which deeds are produced. And what are the three? Freedom from covetousness is a condition under which deeds are produced; freedom from hatred is a condition under which deeds are produced; freedom from infatuation is a condition under which deeds are produced.

When a man's deeds, O priests, are performed without covetousness, arise without covetousness, are occasioned without covetousness, originate without covetousness, then, inasmuch as covetousness is gone, those deeds are abandoned, uprooted, pulled out of the ground like a palmyra-tree, and become non-existent and not liable to spring up again in the future.

When a man's deeds, O priests, are performed without hatred, . . . are performed without infatuation, arise without infatuation, are occasioned without infatuation, originate without infatuation, then, inasmuch as infatuation is gone, those deeds are abandoned, uprooted, pulled out of the ground like a palmyra-tree, and become non-existent and not liable to spring up again in the future.

It is like seed, O priests, that is uninjured, undecayed, unharmed by wind or heat, and is sound, and advantageously sown; if some one then burn it with fire and reduce it to soot, and having reduced it to soot were then to scatter it to the winds, or throw it into a swift-flowing river, then, O priests, will that seed be abandoned, uprooted, pulled out of the ground like a palmyra-tree, and become non-existent and not liable to spring up again in the future. In exactly the same way, O priests, when a man's deeds are performed without covetousness, arise without covetousness, are occasioned without covetousness, originate without covetousness, then, inasmuch as covetousness is gone, those deeds are abandoned, uprooted, pulled out of the ground like a palmyra-tree, and become non-existent and not liable to spring up again in the future; when a man's deeds are performed without hatred, . . . without infatuation, arise without infatuation, are occasioned without infatuation, originate without infatuation, then, inasmuch as infatuation is gone, those deeds are abandoned, uprooted, pulled out of the ground like a palmyra-tree, and become non-existent and not liable to spring up again in the future.

These, O priests, are the three conditions under which deeds are produced.

> A wise priest knows he now must reap
> The fruits of deeds of former births.
> For be they many or but few,
> Deeds done in cov'tousness or hate,
> Or through infatuation's power,
> Must bear their needful consequence.

Hence not to cov'tousness, nor hate,
Nor to infatuation's power
The wise priest yields, but knowledge seeks
And leaves the way to punishment.

2.—Translated from the Añguttara-Nikāya (iii. 99[1])

"O priests, if any one says that a man must reap according to his deeds, in that case, O priests, there is no religious life, nor is any opportunity afforded for the entire extinction of misery. But if any one says, O priests, that the reward a man reaps accords with his deeds, in that case, O priests, there is a religious life, and opportunity is afforded for the entire extinction of misery.

"We may have the case, O priests, of an individual who does some slight deed of wickedness which brings him to hell, or, again, O priests, we may have the case of another individual who does the same slight deed of wickedness, and expiates it in the present life, though it may be in a way which appears to him not slight but grievous.

"What kind of individual, O priests, is he whose slight deed of wickedness brings him to hell?—Whenever, O priests, an individual is not proficient in the management of his body, is not proficient in the precepts, is not proficient in concentration, is not proficient in wisdom, and is limited and bounded, and abides in what is finite and evil: such an individual, O priests, is he whose slight deed of wickedness brings him to hell.

"What kind of individual, O priests, is he who does the same slight deed of wickedness, and expiates it in the present life, though it may be in a way which appears to him not slight but grievous?—Whenever, O priests, an individual is proficient in the management of his body, is proficient in the precepts, is proficient in concentration, is proficient in wisdom, and is not limited, nor bounded, and abides in the universal: such an individual, O priests, is he who does the same slight deed of wickedness, and expiates it in the present life, though it may be in a way which appears to him not slight but grievous.

"It is as if, O priests, a man were to put a lump of salt into a small cup of water. What think ye, O priests? Would now the small amount of water in this cup be made salt and undrinkable by the lump of salt?"

"Yes, Reverend Sir."

"And why?"

"Because, Reverend Sir, there was but a small amount of water in the cup, and so it was made salt and undrinkable by the lump of salt."

"It is as if, O priests, a man were to throw a lump of salt into the river Ganges. What think ye, O priests? Would now the river Ganges be made salt and undrinkable by the lump of salt?"

"Nay, verily, Reverend Sir."

"And why not?"

"Because, Reverend Sir, the mass of water in the river Ganges is great, and so is not made salt and undrinkable by the lump of salt."

"In exactly the same way, O priests, we may have the case of an individual who does some slight deed of wickedness which brings him to hell; or, again, O priests, we may have the case of another individual who does the same slight deed of wickedness, and expiates it in the present life, though it may be in a way which appears to him not slight but grievous.

[Repetition of paragraphs 3 and 4, above.]

"We may have, O priests, the case of one who is cast into prison for a half-penny, for a penny, or for a hundred pence;

or, again, O priests, we may have the case of one who is not cast into prison for a half-penny, for a penny, or for a hundred pence.

"Who, O priests, is cast into prison for a half-penny, for a penny, or for a hundred pence?

"Whenever, O priests, any one is poor, needy, and indigent: he, O priests, is cast into prison for a half-penny, for a penny, or for a hundred pence.

"Who, O priests, is not cast into prison for a half-penny, for a penny, or for a hundred pence?

"Whenever, O priests, any one is rich, wealthy, and affluent: he, O priests, is not cast into prison for a half-penny, for a penny, or for a hundred pence.

"In exactly the same way, O priests, we may have the case of an individual who does some slight deed of wickedness which brings him to hell; or, again, O priests, we may have the case of another individual who does the same slight deed of wickedness, and expiates it in the present life, though it may be in a way which appears to him not slight but grievous.

[Repetition of paragraphs 3 and 4, above.]

"Just as, O priests, a butcher and killer of rams will smite one man if he steal a ram, and will bind him, and burn him, and wreak his pleasure on him; and another who steals a ram, he will not attack, nor bind him, nor burn him, nor wreak his pleasure on him.

"Who is he, O priests, whom a butcher and killer of rams will smite if he steal a ram, and will bind him, and burn him, and wreak his pleasure on him?

"Whenever, O priests, the robber is poor, needy, and indigent: him, O priests, a butcher and killer of rams will smite if he steal a ram, and will bind him, and burn him, and wreak his pleasure on him.

"Who is he, O priests, whom a butcher and killer of rams

will not smite if he steal a ram, nor bind him, nor burn him, nor wreak his pleasure on him?

"Whenever, O priests, the robber is rich, wealthy, and affluent, a king, or a king's minister: him, O priests, a butcher and killer of rams will not smite if he steal a ram, nor bind him, nor burn him, nor wreak his pleasure on him. On the contrary, he will stretch out his joined palms, and make supplication, saying, 'Sir, give me the ram, or the price of the ram.'

"In exactly the same way, O priests, we may have the case of an individual who does some slight deed of wickedness which brings him to hell; or, again, O priests, we may have the case of another individual who does the same slight deed of wickedness, and expiates it in the present life, though it may be in a way which appears to him not slight but grievous.

[Repetition of paragraphs 3 and 4, above.]

"O priests, if any one were to say that a man must reap according to his deeds, in that case, O priests, there is no religious life, nor is any opportunity afforded for the entire extinction of misery. But if any one says, O priests, that the reward a man reaps accords with his deeds, in that case, O priests, there is a religious life, and opportunity is afforded for the entire extinction of misery."

GOOD AND BAD KARMA

Translated from the Samyutta-Nikāya (iii, 2. 10[1])

THUS have I heard.

On a certain occasion The Blessed One was dwelling at Sāvatthi in Jetavana monastery in Anāthapindika's Park.

Then drew near king Pasenadi the Kosalan, at an unusual time of day, to where The Blessed One was; and having drawn near and greeted The Blessed One, he sat down respectfully at one side. And king Pasenadi the Kosalan bang seated respectfully at one side, The Blessed One spoke to him as follows:

"Pray, whence have you come, great king, at this unusual time of day?"

"Reverend Sir, a householder who was treasurer in Sāvatthi has just died leaving no son, and I have come from transferring his property to my royal palace; and, Reverend Sir, he had ten million pieces of gold, and silver beyond all reckoning. But this householder, Reverend Sir, would eat sour gruel and kanājaka, and the clothes he wore were made of hemp . . . , and the conveyance in which he rode was a broken-down chariot with an umbrella of leaves."

"Even so, great king! Even so, great king! Formerly, great king, that householder and treasurer gave food in alms to a Private Buddha named Tagarasikkhi. But after he had given the order, saying, 'Give food to this monk,' and had risen from his seat and departed, he repented him of the gift and said to himself, 'It would have been better if my slaves or my servants had had this food.' And, moreover, he mur-

dered his brother's only son for the sake of the inheritance.
Now whereas, great king, that householder and treasurer
gave food in alms to the Private Buddha Tagarasikkhi, as
the fruit of this deed he was born seven times in a higher
state of existence, into a heavenly world; and as a further result of this deed he has held the treasurership seven times
here in Sāvatthi. And whereas, great king, that householder
and treasurer repented him of the gift, and said to himself,
'It would have been better if my slaves or my servants had
had this food,' as the result of this sinful thought his mind
has been averse to sumptuous food, to sumptuous clothing,
to sumptuous equipages, to a sumptuous gratification of
the five senses. And whereas, great king, the treasurer mur-
dered his brother's only son for the sake of the inheritance,
as a result of this deed he has suffered in hell for many
years, for many hundreds of years, for many thousands of
years, for many hundreds of thousands of years; and as a
further result of this deed he has now for the seventh time
died without leaving any son and forfeited his property
into the royal treasury. But now, great king, the former merit
of this treasurer has become exhausted, and no new merit
has been accumulated, and at the present time, great king,
the treasurer is suffering in the Mahā-Roruva hell."

"Reverend Sir, has the treasurer been reborn in the Mahā-
Roruva hell?"

"Yes, great king. The Treasurer has been reborn in the
Mahā-Roruva hell."

"Nor grain, nor wealth, nor store of gold and silver,
Not one amongst his women-folk and children,
Nor slave, domestic, hired man,
Nor any one that eats his bread,
Can follow him who leaves this life,
But all things must be left behind.

"But every deed a man performs,
With body, or with voice, or mind,
'T is this that he can call his own,
This with him take as he goes hence.
This is what follows after him,
And like a shadow ne'er departs.

"Let all, then, noble deeds perform,
A treasure-store for future weal;
For merit gained this life within,
Will yield a blessing in the next."

REBIRTH IS NOT TRANSMIGRATION

1.—Translated from the Milindapañha (71[16])

SAID the king: "Bhante Nāgasena, does rebirth take place without anything transmigrating [passing over]?"

"Yes, your majesty. Rebirth takes place without anything transmigrating."

"How, bhante Nāgasena, does rebirth take place without anything transmigrating? Give an illustration."

"Suppose, your majesty, a man were to light a light from another light; pray, would the one light have passed over [transmigrated] to the other light?"

"Nay, verily, bhante."

"In exactly the same way, your majesty, does rebirth take place without anything transmigrating."

Give another illustration."

"Do you remember, your majesty, having learnt, when you were a boy, some verse or other from your professor of poetry?"

"Yes, bhante."

"Pray, your majesty, did the verse pass over [transmigrate] to you from your teacher?"

"Nay, verily, bhante."

"In exactly the same way, your majesty, does rebirth take place without anything transmigrating."

"You are an able man, bhante Nāgasena."

2.—Translated from the Milindapañha (46[5])

"Bhante Nāgasena," said the king, "what is it that is born into the next existence?"

"Your majesty," said the elder, "it is name and form that is born into the next existence."

"Is it this same name and form that is born into the next existence?"

"Your majesty, it is not this same name and form that is born into the next existence; but with this name and form, your majesty, one does a deed—it may be good, or it may be wicked—and by reason of this deed another name and form is born into the next existence."

"Bhante, if it is not this same name and form that is born into the next existence, is one not freed from one's evil deeds?"

"If one were not born into another existence," said the elder, "one would be freed from one's evil deeds; but, your majesty, inasmuch as one is born into another existence, therefore is one not freed from one's evil deeds."

"Give an illustration."

"Your majesty, it is as if a man were to take away another man's mangoes, and the owner of the mangoes were to seize him, and show him to the king, and say, 'Sire, this man hath taken away my mangoes;' and the other were to say, 'Sire, I did not take away this man's mangoes. The mangoes which this man planted were different mangoes from those which I took away. I am not liable to punishment.' Pray, your majesty, would the man be liable to punishment?"

"Assuredly, bhante, would he be liable to punishment."

"For what reason?"

"Because, in spite of what he might say, he would be liable to punishment for the reason that the last mangoes derived from the first mangoes."

"In exactly the same way, your majesty, with this name and form one does a deed—it may be good, or it may be wicked—and by reason of this deed another name and form is born into the next existence. Therefore is one not freed from one's evil deeds."

"Give another illustration."

"Your majesty, it is as if a man were to take away the rice of another man, . . . were to take away the sugar-cane, . . . Your majesty, it is as if a man were to light a fire in the winter-time and warm himself, and were to go off without putting it out. And then the fire were to burn another man's field, and the owner of the field were to seize him, and show him to the king, and say, 'Sire, this man has burnt up my field;' and the other were to say, 'Sire, I did not set this man's field on fire. The fire which I failed to put out was a different one from the one which has burnt up this man's field. I am not liable to punishment.' Pray, your majesty, would the man be liable to punishment?"

"Assuredly, bhante, would he be liable to punishment."

"For what reason?"

"Because, in spite of what he might say, the man would be liable to punishment for the reason that the last fire derived from the first fire."

"In exactly the same way, your majesty, with this name and form one does a deed—it may be good, or it may be wicked—and by reason of this deed another name and form is born into the next existence. Therefore is one not freed from one's evil deeds."

"Give another illustration."

"Your majesty, it is as if a man were to ascend to the top story of a house with a light, and eat there; and the light in burning were to set fire to the thatch; and the thatch in burning were to set fire to the house; and the house in burning were to set fire to the village; and the people of the village were to seize him, and say, 'Why, O man, did you set fire to the village?' and he were to say, 'I did not set fire to the village. The fire of the lamp by whose light I ate was a different one from the one which set fire to the village;' and they, quarreling, were to come to you. Whose cause, your majesty, would you sustain?"

"That of the people of the village, bhante."

"And why?"

"Because, in spite of what the man might say, the latter fire sprang from the former."

"In exactly the same way, your majesty, although the name and form which is born into the next existence is different from the name and form which is to end at death, nevertheless, it is sprung from it. Therefore is one not freed from one's evil deeds."

"Give another illustration."

"Your majesty, it is as if a man were to choose a young girl in marriage, and having paid the purchase-money, were to go off; and she subsequently were to grow up and become marriageable; and then another man were to pay the purchase-money for her, and marry her; and the first man were to return, and say, 'O man, why did you marry my wife?' and the other were to say, 'I did not marry your wife. The young, tender girl whom you chose in marriage, and for whom you paid purchase-money, was a different person from this grown-up and marriageable girl whom I have chosen in marriage, and for whom I have paid purchase-money;' and they, quarreling, were to come to you. Whose cause, your majesty, would you sustain?"

"That of the first man."

"And why?"

"Because, in spite of what the second man might say, the grown-up girl sprang from the other."

"In exactly the same way, your majesty, although the

name and form which is born into the next existence is different from the name and form which is to end at death,
nevertheless, it is sprung from it. Therefore is one not freed
from one's evil deeds."

"Give another illustration."

"Your majesty it is as if a man were to buy from a cowherd a pot of milk, and were to leave it with the cowherd,
and go off, thinking he would come the next day and take
it. And on the next day it were to turn into sour cream; and
the man were to come back, and say, 'Give me the pot of
milk.' And the other were to show him the sour cream; and
the first man were to say, 'I did not buy sour cream from
you. Give me the pot of milk.' And the cowherd were to say,
'While you were gone, your milk turned into sour cream;'
and they, quarreling, were to come to you. Whose cause,
your majesty, would you sustain?"

"That of the cowherd, bhante."

"And why?"

"Because, in spite of what the man might say, the one
sprang from the other."

"In exactly the same way, your majesty, although the
name and form which is born into the next existence is different from the name and form which is to end at death,
nevertheless, it is sprung from it. Therefore is one not freed
from one's evil deeds."

"You are an able man, bhante Nāgasena."

3.—Translated from the Visuddhi-Magga (chap. xvii.)

It is only elements of being possessing a dependence that
arrive at a new existence: none transmigrated from the last
existence, nor are they in the new existence without causes
contained in the old. By this is said that it is only elements

of being, with form or without, but possessing a dependence, that arrive at a new existence. There is no entity, no living principle; no elements of being transmigrated from the last existence into the present one; nor, on the other hand, do they appear in the present existence without causes in that one. This we will now make plain by considering birth and death as they occur every day among men.

For when, in any existence, one arrives at the gate of death, either in the natural course of things or through violence; and when, by a concourse of intolerable, death-dealing pains, all the members, both great and small, are loosened and wrenched apart in every joint and ligament; and the body, like a green palm-leaf exposed to the sun, dries up by degrees; and the eye-sight and the other senses fail; and the power of feeling, and the power of thinking, and vitality are making the last stand in the heart—then consciousness residing in that last refuge, the heart, continues to exist by virtue of karma, otherwise called the predispositions. This karma, however, still retains something of what it depends on, and consists of such former deeds as were weighty, much practised, and are now close at hand; or else this karma creates a reflex of itself or of the new mode of life now being entered upon, and it is with this as its object that consciousness continues to exist.

Now while the consciousness still subsists, inasmuch as desire and ignorance have not been abandoned and the evil of the object is hidden by that ignorance, desire inclines the consciousness to the object; and the karma that sprang up along with the consciousness impels it toward the object. This consciousness being in its series thus inclined toward the object by desire, and impelled toward it by karma, like a man who swings himself over a ditch by means of a rope hanging from a tree on the hither bank, quits its first resting-place and continues to subsist in dependence on objects of sense and other things, and either does or does not light on another resting-place created by karma. Here the former consciousness, from its passing out of existence, is called passing away, and the latter, from its being reborn into a new existence, is called rebirth. But it is to be understood that this latter consciousness did not come to the present existence from the previous one, and also that it is only to causes contained in the old existence,—namely, to karma called the predispositions, to inclination, an object, etc.,—that its present appearance is due.

> As illustrations here may serve
> Echoes and other similes.
> Nor sameness, nor diversity,
> Can from that series take their rise.

As illustrations of how consciousness does not come over from the last existence into the present, and how it springs up by means of causes belonging to the former existence, *here may serve echoes*, light the impressions of a seal, and reflections in a mirror. For as echoes, light, the impressions of a seal, and shadows have sound, etc., for their causes, and exist without having come from elsewhere, just so is it with this mind.

Moreover

> *Nor sameness, nor diversity,*
> *Can from that series take their rise.*

For if, in a continuous series, an absolute sameness obtained, then could sour cream not arise from milk; while, on the other hand, if there were an absolute diversity, then could not a milk-owner obtain sour cream. The same argument holds good in regard to all causes and effects. This being so, it would be more correct not to use the popular mode of stating the case, but that would not be desirable. Therefore, we must merely guard ourselves from supposing that there is here either an absolute satneness or an absolute diversity. Here some one will say,

"This explanation is not a good one. For is it not true that if there be no transmigration, and both the Groups and the fruitful karma which belong to this existence in the world of men cease, nor arrive in the new existence, the fruit of this karma would then be borne by a different thing from that which produced the karma itself? If the reaper ceased to exist, it would not be he experienced the fruit. Therefore this position is not good."

The following quotation will answer this:

"The series which doth bear a fruit,
Is not the same nor something else.
The fabricating power in seeds
Will show the meaning of this word."

For when the *fruit* arises in a *series*, as absolute sameness and absolute diversity are both excluded, it cannot be said that the fruit is borne by the *same* thing *nor* yet by *something else*.

The fabricating power in seeds will show this. For when the fabricating power in the seed of mangoes and other plants operate, inasmuch as any particular kind of fruit is dependent on the previous part of its series, it cannot come from other seeds, nor in dependence on other fabricating powers; nor yet is it those other seeds, or those other fabricating powers, which arrive at fruition. Such is to be understood to be the nature of the present case. Also when education,

training, and medicaments have been applied to the body
of a young person, the fruit will appear in after time in the
mature body, etc. Thus is the sense to be understood.

Now as to what was said, "If the reaper ceased to exist, it
would not be he experienced the fruit," consider the following:

> "As when 't is said, 'The tree bears fruit,'
> As soon as fruit on it appears;
> Just so the Groups are reapers called,
> As soon as karma's fruit springs up."

Just as in the case of those elements of being which go
under the name of tree, as soon as at any point the fruit
springs up, *it is* then *said, "The tree bears fruit,"* or, "The tree
has fructified"—so also in the case of those *Groups* which go
under the name of "god" or "man," when a fruition of happiness or misery springs up at any point, then it is said,
"That god or man is happy or miserable." Therefore is it
that we have here no need of any other *reaper.*

4.—Translated from the Visuddhi-Magga (chap. xvii.)

He, then, that has no clear idea of death and does not master the fact that death everywhere consists in the dissolution
of the Groups, he comes to a variety of conclusions, such as,
"A living entity dies and transmigrates into another body."

He that has no clear idea of rebirth and does not master
the fact that the appearance of the Groups everywhere constitutes rebirth, he comes to a variety of conclusions, such
as, "A living entity is born and has obtained a new body."

5.—Translated from the Visuddhi-Magga (chap. xxi.)

Therefore have the ancients said:

"'The Groups break up, and only they,' the wise say,
'And death consisteth in their dissolution.'
The thoughtful man of insight sees them vanish;
They're like the jewel shattered by the diamond."

DEATH'S MESSENGERS

1.—Translated from the Aṅguttara-Nikāya (iii. 35[1])

DEATH has three messengers, O priests. And what are the three?

Suppose, O priests, one does evil with his body, does evil with his voice, does evil with his mind. Having done evil with his body, done evil with his voice, and done evil with his mind, he arrives after the dissolution of the body, after death, at a place of punishment, a place of suffering, perdition, hell. Then, O priests, the guardians of hell seize him by the arms at every point, and they show him to Yama, the ruler of the dead, saying,

"Sire, this man did not do his duty to his friends, to his parents, to the monks, or to the Brahmans, nor did he honor his elders among his kinsfolk. Let your majesty inflict punishment upon him."

Then, O priests, king Yama questions, sounds, and addresses him touching the first of death's messengers.

"O man! Did you not see the first of death's messengers visibly appear among men?"

He replies, "Lord, I did not."

Then, O priests, king Yama says to him, "O man! Did you not see among men a woman or a man, eighty or ninety or a hundred years of age, decrepit, crooked as the curved rafter of a gable roof, bowed down, leaning on a staff, trembling as he walked, miserable, with youth long fled, broken-toothed, gray-haired and nearly bald, tottering, with wrinkled brow, and blotched with freckles?"

He replies, "Lord, I did."

Then, O priests, king Yama says to him, "O man! Did it not occur to you, being a person of mature intelligence and years, 'I also am subject to old age, and in no way exempt. Come now! I will act nobly with body, voice, and mind'?"

He replies, "Lord, I could not. Lord, I did not think."

Then, O priests, king Yama says to him, "O man! Through thoughtlessness you failed to act nobly with body, voice, and mind. Verily, it shall be done unto you, O man, in accordance with your thoughtlessness. And it was not your mother who did this wickedness, nor was it your father, nor your brother, nor your sister, nor your friends and companions, nor your relatives and kinsfolk, nor the deities, nor the monks and Brahmans; but it was you yourself who did this wickedness, and you alone shall feel its consequences."

Then, O priests, when king Yama has questioned, sounded, and addressed him touching the first of death's messengers, he questions, sounds, and addresses him touching the second of death's messengers.

"O man! Did you not see the second of death's messengers visibly appear among men?"

He replies, "Lord, I did not."

Then, O priests, king Yama says to him, "O man! Did you not see among men women or men, diseased, suffering, grievously sick, rolling in their own filth, who when lying down had to be lifted up by others, and by others had to be laid down again?"

He replies, "Lord, I did."

Then, O priests, king Yama says to him, "O man! Did it not occur to you, being a person of mature intelligence and years, 'I also am subject to disease, and in no way exempt. Come now! I will act nobly with body, voice, and mind'?"

He replies, "Lord, I could not. Lord, I did not think."

Then, O priests, king Yama says to him, "O man! Through

thoughtlessness you failed to act nobly with body, voice, and mind. Verily, it shall be done unto you, O man, in accordance with your thoughtlessness. And it was not your mother who did this wickedness, nor was it your father, nor your brother, nor your sister, nor your friends and companions, nor your relatives and kinsfolk, nor the deities, nor the monks and Brahmans; but it was you yourself who did this wickedness, and you alone shall feel its consequences."

Then, O priests, when king Yama has questioned, sounded, and addressed him touching the second of death's messengers, he questions, sounds, and addresses him touching the third of death's messengers.

"O man! Did you not see the third of death's messengers visibly appear among men?"

He replies, "Lord, I did not."

Then, O priests, king Yama says to him, "O man! Did you not see among men a woman or a man that has been one day dead, or two days dead, or three days dead, and had become swollen, black, and full of putridity?"

He replies, "Lord, I did."

Then, O priests, king Yama says to him, "O man! Did it not occur to you, being a person of mature intelligence and years, 'I also am subject to death, and in no way exempt. Come now! I will act nobly with body, voice, and mind'?"

He replies, "Lord, I could not. Lord, I did not think."

Then, O priests, king Yama says to him, "O man! Through thoughtlessness you failed to act nobly with body, voice, and mind. Verily, it shall be done unto you, O man, in accordance with your thoughtlessness. And it was not your mother who did this wickedness, nor was it your father, nor your brother, nor your sister, nor your friends and companions, nor your relatives and kinsfolk, nor the deities, nor the monks and Brahmans; but it was you yourself who did this wickedness, and you alone shall feel its consequences."

Then, O priests, when king Yama has questioned, sounded, and addressed him touching the third of death's messengers, he becomes silent.

Then, O priests, the guardians of hell inflict on him the torture called the fivefold pinion: they force a heated iron stake through his hand; they force a heated iron stake through his other hand; they force a heated iron stake through his foot; they force a heated iron stake through his other foot; they force a heated iron stake through the middle of his breast. There he experiences grievous, severe, sharp, and bitter pains; but he does not die so long as that wickedness is unexhausted.

Then, O priests, the guardians of hell lay him down, and hack him with axes. There he experiences grievous, severe, sharp, and bitter pains; but he does not die so long as that wickedness is unexhausted.

Then, O priests, the guardians of hell place him feet up, head down, and hack him with hatchets. There he experiences grievous, severe, sharp, and bitter pains; but he does not die so long as that wickedness is unexhausted.

Then, O priests, the guardians of hell harness him to a chariot, and they make him go forward and they make him go back over ground that is blazing, flaming, and glowing. There he experiences grievous, severe, sharp, and bitter pains; but he does not die so long as that wickedness is unexhausted.

Then, O priests, the guardians of hell make him ascend and make him descend an immense, blazing, flaming, and glowing mountain of live coals. There he experiences grievous, severe, sharp, and bitter pains; but he does not die so long as that wickedness is unexhausted.

Then, O priests, the guardians of hell take him feet up, head down, and throw him into a heated iron kettle that is blazing, flaming, and glowing. There he cooks and sizzles.

And while he there cooks and sizzles, he goes once upwards, once downwards, and once sideways. There he experiences grievous, severe, sharp, and bitter pains; but he does not die so long as that wickedness is unexhausted. Then, O priests, the guardians of hell throw him into the chiefest of the hells. Now this chiefest of the hells, O priests, is

> Symmetrical and square in shape,
> Four-gated, into parts laid off.
> Of iron is its bounding wall,
> An iron roof doth close it in;
> And of its glowing iron floor
> The light with dazzling brilliancy
> Spreads for a hundred leagues around,
> And ever and for ay abides.

In former times, O priests, king Yama thought to himself, "All they, alas, who are guilty of wicked deeds in the world must suffer such horrible and manifold torture! O that I may become a man and a Tathāgata arise in the world, a holy, Supreme Buddha, and that I may sit at the feet of The Blessed One and The Blessed One teach me the Doctrine, and I come to understand the Doctrine of The Blessed One!"

Now this, O priests, that I tell you, I did not get from any one else, be he monk or Brahman; but, O priests, what I by myself, unassisted, have known, and seen, and learnt, that I tell you.

> All they who thoughtless are, nor heed,
> What time death's messengers appear,
> Must long the pangs of suffering feel
> In some base body habiting.
> But all those good and holy men,
> What time they see death's messengers,

Behave not thoughtless, but give heed
To what the Noble Doctrine says;
And in attachment frighted see
Of birth and death the fertile source,
And from attachment free themselves,
Thus birth and death extinguishing,
Secure and happy ones are they,
Released from all this fleeting show;
Exempted from all sin and fear,
All misery have they overcome.

2.—Reprinted from Mrs. Piozzi's (Thrale's)
Autobiography (ed. Hayward, Ticknor and Fields,
Boston, 1861), vol. ii. p. 247

THE THREE WARNINGS

A TALE

The tree of deepest root is found
Least willing still to quit the ground;
'T was therefore said by ancient sages,
That love of life increased with years.
So much, that in our latter stages,
When pains grow sharp and sickness rages,
The greatest love of life appears.
This greatest affection to believe,
Which all confess, but few perceive,
If old affections cants prevail,
Be pleased to hear a modern tale.
When sports went round, and all were gay,
On neighbor Dobson's wedding-day,
Death called aside the jocund groom,

With him into another room;
And looking grave, you must, says he,
Quit your sweet bride, and come with me.
With you, and quit my Susan's side?
With you! the hapless husband cried:
Young as I am; 't is monstrous hard;
Besides, in truth, I'm not prepared;
My thoughts on other matters go,
This is my wedding night, you know.
What more he urged I have not heard,
His reasons could not well be stronger,
So Death the poor delinquent spared,
And left to live a little longer.
Yet calling up a serious look,
His hour-glass trembled while he spoke,
Neighbor, he said, farewell. No more
Shall Death disturb your mirthful hour,
And further, to avoid all blame
Of cruelty upon my name,
To give you time for preparation,
And fit you for your future station,
Three several warnings you shall have
Before you're summoned to the grave:
Willing, for once, I'll quit my prey,
And grant a kind reprieve;
In hopes you'll have no more to say
But when I call again this way,
Well pleased the world will leave.
To these conditions both consented,
And parted perfectly contented.
What next the hero of our tale befell,
How long he lived, how wise, how well,
How roundly he pursued his course,
And smoked his pipe, and stroked his horse,

The willing muse shall tell:
He chaffered then, he bought, he sold,
Nor once perceived his growing old,
Nor thought of Death as near;
His friends not false, his wife no shrew,
Many his gains, his children few,
He passed his hours in peace;
But while he viewed his wealth increase,
While thus along life's dusty road
The beaten track content he trod,
Old time whose haste no mortal spares
Uncalled, unheeded, unawares,
Brought him on his eightieth year.
And now one night in musing mood,
As all alone he sate,
Th' unwelcome messenger of fate
Once more before him stood.
Half stilled with anger and surprise,
So soon returned! old Dobson cries.
So soon, d' ye call it! Death replies:
Surely, my friend, you're but in jest;
Since I was here before
'T is six-and-thirty years at least,
And you are now fourscore.
So much the worse, the clown rejoined,
To spare the aged would be kind;
However, see your search be legal
And your authority,—Is 't regal?
Else you are come on a fool's errand,
With but a secretary's warrant.
Besides, you promised me three warnings,
Which I have looked for nights and mornings;
But for that loss of time and ease
I can recover damages.

I know, cries Death, that at the best,
I seldom am a welcome guest;
But don't be captious, friend, at least;
I little thought you'd still be able
To stump about your farm and stable;
Your years have run to a great length,
I wish you joy though of your strength.
Hold, says the farmer, not so fast,
I have been lame these four years past.
And no great wonder, Death replies;
However, you still keep your eyes,
And sure to see one's loves and friends,
For legs and arms would make amends.
Perhaps, says Dobson, so it might,
But, latterly, I've lost my sight.
This is a shocking story, faith,
Yet there's some comfort still, says Death;
Each strives your sadness to amuse,
I warrant you have all the news.
There's none, cries he, and if there were,
I've grown so deaf, I could not hear.
Nay then, the spectre stern rejoined,
These are unjustifiable yearnings;
If you are lame and deaf and blind,
You've had your three sufficient warnings
So come along, no more we'll part:
He said, and touched him with his dart;
And now old Dobson, turning pale,
Yields to his fate,—so ends my tale.

THE DEVOTED WIFE

Translated from the Dhammapada, and
from Buddhaghosa's comment

While eagerly man culls life's flowers,
With all his faculties intent,
Of pleasure still insatiate—
Death comes and overpowereth him.

"WHILE eagerly man culls life's flowers." This doctrinal instruction was given by The Teacher while dwelling at Sāvatthi, and it was concerning a woman called Husband-honorer. The affair began in the Heaven of the Suite of the Thirty-three.

They say that a god of that heaven named Garland-wearer went to his pleasure-grounds in company with a thousand celestial nymphs. Five hundred of these goddesses ascended trees and threw down flowers, while five hundred picked up the flowers that were thrown down and decked the god therewith. One of these goddesses, while on the bough of a tree, fell from that existence, her body vanishing like the flame of a lamp.

Then she was conceived in a high-caste family of Sāvatthi, and was born with a reminiscence of her previous existences. And saying to herself, "I am the wife of the god Garland-wearer," she made offerings of perfumes, garlands, and the like, with the prayer that in her next rebirth she might again be with her husband. And when at the age of sixteen years she married into another family, with ticket-food, and fort-nightly food, she continued to give alms, saying, "May this prove efficacious in bringing about my rebirth with my husband."

Thereupon the priests gave her the name of Husband-honorer, for they said: "She works early and late, and her only desire is for her husband."

Husband-honorer continually took care of the hall where the priests sat. She brought forward the drinking water, and spread out the mats to sit on. And when other people were desirous of giving ticket-food and other alms, they would bring it to her, and say, "Dear lady, prepare this for the congregation of the priests." And by going to and fro in this manner, she acquired the fifty-six salutary qualities, all at one time.

Then she conceived, and at the end of ten lunar months she brought forth a son; and when he was old enough to walk, another, until she had four sons.

One day, after she had given alms and offerings, and had listened to the Doctrine, and kept the precepts, she died toward night-fall from a sudden disease, and was reborn into the presence of her husband.

The other goddesses had continued to deck the god throughout the whole interval.

"We have not seen you since morning," said the god. "Where have you been?"

"I fell from this existence, my lord."

"Are you in earnest?"

"It was precisely so, my lord."

"Where were you born?"

"At Sāvatthi, in a family of high caste."

"How long were you there?"

"My lord, at the end of ten months I issued from my mother's womb, and at the age of sixteen years I married into another family; and having borne four sons, and having given gifts and done other meritorious deeds with the prayer that I might again be with you, I have been born into your presence."

"How long is the life of men?"

"Only a hundred years."

"Is that all?"

"Yes, my lord."

"If that is the length of life to which men are born, pray, now, do they pass the time asleep and reckless, or do they give gifts and do other meritorious deeds?"

"Nothing of the kind, my lord. Men are always reckless, as if they were born to a life of an incalculable number of years, and were never to grow old and die."

At this the god Garland-wearer became exceedingly agitated.

"Men, it appears, are born to a life of only one hundred years, yet they recklessly lie down and sleep away their time. When will they ever get free from misery?"

A hundred of our years make one day and night of the Gods of the Suite of the Thirty-three; thirty such days and nights their month; and twelve such months their year. And the length of their lives is a thousand such celestial years, or in human notation thirty-six million years. Thus for that god not one day has passed; but like a moment had the interval seemed to him. And thus he thought, "Recklessness for short-lived men is extremely unsuitable."

On the next day, when the priests entered the village, they found the hall had not been looked after; the mats had not been spread, and the drinking water had not been placed. Then they inquired,

"Where is Husband-honorer?"

"Reverend sirs, how could you expect to see her? Yesterday, after your worships had eaten and departed, she died at even-tide."

When the priests heard this, the unconverted among them, calling to mind her benefactions, were unable to restrain their tears, while those in whom depravity had come to an end had their elements of being agitated.

After breakfast they returned to the monastery, and made inquiry of The Teacher:

"Reverend Sir, Husband-honorer worked early and late doing many kinds of meritorious deeds, and prayed only for her husband. Now she is dead. Where, pray, has she been reborn?"

"With her husband, O priests."

"But, Reverend Sir, she is not with her husband."

"O priests, it was not this husband she was praying for. She had a husband named Garland-wearer, a God of the Suite of the Thirty-three, and fell from that existence while he was decorating himself with flowers. Now she has returned and been born again at his side."

"Reverend Sir, is it really so?"

"Assuredly, O priests."

"Alas, Reverend Sir, how very short is the life of all creatures! In the morning she waited on us, and in the evening a disease attacked her, and she died."

"Assuredly, O priests," said The Teacher, "the life of creatures is indeed short. And thus it is that death gets creatures into his power, and drags them away howling and weeping, and still unsated in their senses and lusts."

So saying, he pronounced the following stanza:

> "While eagerly man culls life's flowers,
> With all his faculties intent,
> Of pleasure still insatiate—
> Death comes and overpowereth him."

THE HARE-MARK IN
THE MOON

Translated from the Jātaka (iii. 51[10]), and
constituting Birth-Story 316

"SOME red-fish have I, seven in all." This was related by The
Teacher while dwelling in Jetavana monastery; and it was
concerning a donation of all the requisites to the congregation of the priests.

It seems that a householder of Sāvatthi prepared a donation of all the requisites for The Buddha and for the Order.
At the door of his house he had a pavilion built and gotten
ready, and having invited The Buddha and the congregation of the priests, he made them sit down on costly seats
which had been spread for them in the pavilion, and gave
them an excellent repast of savory dishes. Then he invited
them again for the next day, and again for the next, until he
had invited them seven times. And on the seventh day he
made the donation of all the requisites to The Buddha and
to five hundred priests.

At the end of the breakfast The Teacher returned thanks
and said,

"Layman, it is fitting that you thus manifest a hearty zeal;
for this alms-giving was also the custom of the wise of old
time. For the wise of old time surrendered their own lives to
chance suppliants, and gave their own flesh to be eaten."

Then, at the request of the householder, he related the by-
gone occurrence:—

Once upon a time, when Brahmadatta was ruling at
Benares, the Future Buddha was born as a hare, and dwelt

115

in a wood. Now on one side of this wood was a mountain, on another a river, and on another a border village. And there were three other animals that were his comrades—a monkey, a jackal, and an otter. These four wise creatures dwelt together, catching their prey each in his own hunting ground, and at night resorting together. And the wise hare would exhort the other three, and teach them the Doctrine, saying, "Give alms, keep the precepts, and observe fast-days." Then the three would approve of his admonition, and go each to his own lair in the thicket, and spend the night.

Time was going by in this manner, when one day the Future Buddha looked up into the sky and saw the moon, and perceived that the next day would be fast-day. Then said he to the others,

"To-morrow is fast-day. Do you three keep the precepts and observe the day; and as alms given while keeping the precepts bring great reward, if any suppliants present themselves, give them to eat of your own food."

"Very well," said they, and passed the night in their lairs.

On the next day the otter started out early, and went to the banks of the Ganges to hunt for prey. Now a fisherman had caught seven red-fish and strung them on a vine, and buried them in the sand on the banks of the Ganges, and had then gone on down-stream catching fish as he went. The otter smelt the fishy odor, and scraping away the sand, perceived the fish and drew them out. Then he called out three times, "Does any one own these?" and when he saw no owner, he bit hold of the vine with his teeth, and drew them to his lair in the thicket. There he lay down, remembering that he was keeping the precepts, and thinking, "I will eat these at the proper time."

And the jackal also went out to hunt for prey, and found in the hut of a field-watcher two spits of meat, and one iguana, and a jar of sour cream. Then he called out three times, "Does any one own these?" and when he saw no owner, he placed the cord that served as a handle for the jar of sour cream about his neck, took hold of the spits of meat and of the iguana with his teeth, and brought them home, and placed them in his lair in the thicket. Then he lay down, remembering that he was keeping the precepts, and thinking, "I will eat these at the proper time."

And the monkey also, entering the forest, fetched home a bunch of mangoes, and placed them in his lair in the thicket. Then he lay down, remembering that he was keeping the precepts, and thinking, "I will eat these at the proper time."

The Future Buddha, however, remained in his thicket, thinking, "At the proper time I will go out and eat dabba[1]-grass." Then he thought,

"If any suppliants come, they will not want to eat grass, and I have no sesamum, rice, or other such food. If any suppliant comes, I will give him of my own flesh."

Such fieriness of zeal in keeping the precepts caused the marble throne of Sakka to grow hot. Then, looking carefully, Sakka discovered the cause, and proposed to himself to try the hare. And disguised as a Brahman, he went first to the lair of the otter.

"Brahman, why stand you there?" said the otter.

Said he, "Pandit, if I could but get something to eat, I would keep fast-day vows, and perform the duties of a monk."

"Very well," said the otter; "I will give you food." And he addressed him with the first stanza:

"Some red-fish have I, seven in all,
Found stranded on the river bank.

[1]Name of various kinds of grasses used for sacrificial purposes.

All these, O Brahman, are my own;
Come eat, and dwell within this wood."

"I will return a little later," said the Brahman; "let the matter rest until to-morrow."

Then he went to the jackal. And the latter also asking, "Why stand you there?" the Brahman answered the same as before.

"Very well," said the jackal; "I will give you some food." And he addressed him with the second stanza:

"A watchman guards the field close by,
His supper have I ta'en away;
Two spits of meat, iguana one,
One dish of butter clarified.
All these, O Brahman, are my own;
Come eat, and dwell within this wood."

"I will return a little later," said the Brahman, "let the matter rest until to-morrow."

Then he went to the monkey. And the latter also asking, "Why stand you there?" the Brahman answered the same as before.

"Very well," said the monkey; "I will give you some food." And he addressed him with the third stanza:

"Ripe mangoes, water clear and cold,
And cool and pleasant woodland shade—
All these, O Brahman, are my own;
Come eat, and dwell within this wood."

"I will return a little later," said the Brahman; "let the matter rest until to-morrow."

Then he went to the wise hare. And he also asking, "Why

stand you there?" the Brahman answered the same as before.

The Future Buddha was delighted. "Brahman," said he,
"you have done well in coming to me for food. To-day I will
give alms such as I never gave before; and you will not have
broken the precepts by destroying life. Go, my friend, and
gather wood, and when you have made a bed of coals,
come and tell me. I will sacrifice my life by jumping into the
bed of live coals. And as soon as my body is cooked, do you
eat of my flesh, and perform the duties of a monk." And he
addressed him with the fourth stanza:

> "The hare no seed of sesamum
> Doth own, nor beans, nor winnowed rice,
> But soon my flesh this fire shall roast;
> Then eat, and dwell within this wood."

When Sakka heard this speech, he made a heap of live
coals by his superhuman power, and came and told the
Future Buddha. The latter rose from his couch of dabba-
grass, and went to the spot. And saying, "If there are any in-
sects in my fur, I must not let them die," he shook himself
three times. Then throwing his whole body into the jaws of
his liberality, he jumped into the bed of coals, as delighted
in mind as a royal flamingo when he alights in a cluster of
lotuses. The fire, however, was unable to make hot so much
as a hair-pore of the Future Buddha's body. He felt as if he
had entered the abode of cold above the clouds.

Then, addressing Sakka, he said,

"Brahman, the fire you have made is exceeding cold, and
is not able to make hot so much as a hair-pore of my body.
What does it mean?"

"Pandit, I am no Brahman; I am Sakka, come to try you."

"Sakka, your efforts are useless; for if all beings who

dwell in the world were to try me in respect of my liberality, they would not discover in me any unwillingness to give." Thus the Future Buddha thundered.

"Wise hare," said then Sakka, "let your virtue be proclaimed to the end of this world-cycle." And taking a mountain, he squeezed it, and with the juice drew the outline of a hare in the disk of the moon. Then in that wood, and in that thicket, he placed the Future Buddha on some tender dabba-grass, and taking leave of him, departed to his own celestial abode.

And these four wise creatures lived happily and harmoniously, and kept the precepts, and observed fast-days, and passed away according to their deeds.

When The Teacher had given this instruction, he expounded the truth, and identified the characters of the Birth-Story: [At the close of the exposition of the truths, the householder who had given all the requisites became established in the fruit of conversion.]

"In that existence the otter was Ananda, the jackal was Moggallāna, the monkey was Sāriputta, while the wise hare was I myself."

The Hare Birth-Story.

THE WAY OF PURITY

Translated from the Visuddhi-Magga (chap. i.)

THEREFORE has The Blessed One said:

"What man his conduct guardeth, and hath wisdom,
And thoughts and wisdom traineth well,
The strenuous and the able priest,
He disentangles all this snarl."

When it is said *hath wisdom*, there is meant a wisdom for which he does not need to strive. For it comes to him through the power of his deeds in a former existence.

The strenuous and the able priest. Perseveringly by means of the above-mentioned heroism, and intelligently through the force of his wisdom, should he *guard* his *conduct*, and *train* himself in the quiescence and insight indicated by the words *thoughts* and *wisdom*.

Thus does The Blessed One reveal the Way of Purity under the heads of conduct, concentration, and wisdom. Thus does he indicate the three disciplines, a thrice noble religion, the advent of the threefold knowledge, etc., the avoidance of the two extremes and the adoption of the middle course of conduct, the means of escape from the lower and other states of existence, the threefold abandonment of the corruptions, the three hostilities, the purification from the three corruptions, and the attainment of conversion and of the other degrees of sanctification.

And how?

By conduct is indicated the discipline in elevated conduct; by concentration, the discipline in elevated thoughts; and by wisdom, the discipline in elevated wisdom.

By conduct, again, is indicated the nobleness of this religion in its beginning. The fact that conduct is the beginning of this religion appears from the passage, "What is the first of the meritorious qualities? Purity of conduct." And again from that other, which begins by saying, "It is the nonperformance of any wickedness." And it is noble because it entails no remorse or other like evils.

By concentration is indicated its nobleness in the middle. The fact that concentration is the middle of this religion appears from the passage which begins by saying, "It is richness in merit." It is noble because it brings one into the possession of the magical powers and other blessings.

By wisdom is indicated its nobleness at the end. The fact that wisdom is the end of this religion appears from the passage,

> "To cleanse and purify the thoughts,
> 'T is this the holy Buddhas teach,"

and from the fact that there is nothing higher than wisdom. It is noble because it brings about imperturbability whether in respect of things pleasant or unpleasant. As it is said:

> "Even as the dense and solid rock
> Cannot be stirred by wind and storm;
> Even so the wise cannot be moved
> By voice of blame or voice of praise."

By conduct, again, is indicated the advent of the threefold knowledge. For by virtuous conduct one acquires the threefold knowledge, but gets no further. By concentration is indicated the advent of the Six High Powers. For by concentration one acquires the Six High Powers, but gets no further. By wisdom is indicated the advent of the four analytical sciences. For by wisdom one acquires the four analytical sciences, and in no other way.

By conduct, again, is indicated the avoidance of the extreme called sensual gratification; by concentration, the avoidance of the extreme called self-torture. By wisdom is indicated the adoption of the middle course of conduct.

By conduct, again, is indicated the means of escape from the lower states of existence; by concentration, the means of escape from the realm of sensual pleasure; by wisdom, the means of escape from every form of existence.

By conduct, again, is indicated the abandonment of the corruption through the cultivation of their opposing virtues, by concentration, the abandonment of the corruptions through their avoidance; by wisdom, the abandonment of the corruptions through their extirpation.

By conduct, again, is indicated the hostility to corrupt acts; by concentration, the hostility to corrupt feelings; by wisdom, the hostility to corrupt propensities.

By conduct, again, is indicated the purification from the corruption of bad practices; by concentration, the purification from the corruption of desire; by wisdom, the purification from the corruption of heresy.

And by conduct, again, is indicated the attainment of conversion, and of once returning; by concentration, the attainment of never returning; by wisdom, the attainment of saintship. For the converted are described as "Perfect in the precepts," as likewise the once returning; but the never returning as "Perfect in concentration," and the saint as "Perfect in wisdom."

Thus are indicated the three disciplines, a thrice noble religion, the advent of the threefold knowledge, etc., the avoid-

ance of the two extremes and the adoption of the middle
course of conduct, the means of escape from the lower and
other states of existence, the threefold abandonment of the
corruptions, the three hostilities, the purification from the
three corruptions, and the attainment of conversion and of
the other degrees of sanctification; and not only these nine
triplets, but also other similar ones.

Now although this *Way of Purity* was thus taught under
the heads of conduct, concentration, and wisdom, and of
the many good qualities comprised in them, yet this with
excessive conciseness; and as, consequently, many would
fail to be benefited, we here give its exposition in detail.

CONCENTRATION

1.—Translated from the Visuddhi-Magga (chap. iii.)

WHAT is concentration? Concentration is manifold and various, and an answer which attempted to be exhaustive would both fail of its purpose and tend to still greater confusion. Therefore we will confine ourselves to the meaning here intended, and say—Concentration is an intentness of meritorious thoughts.

2.—Translated from the Aṅguttara-Nikāya (iii. 88)

And what, O priests, is the discipline in elevated concentration?

Whenever, O priests, a priest, having isolated himself from sensual pleasures, having isolated himself from demeritorious traits, and still exercising reasoning, still exercising reflection, enters upon the first trance, which is produced by isolation and characterized by joy and happiness; when, through the subsidence of reasoning and reflection, and still retaining joy and happiness, he enters upon the second trance, which is an interior tranquilization and intentness of thoughts, and is produced by concentration; when, through the paling of joy, indifferent, contemplative, conscious, and in the experience of bodily happiness—that state which eminent men describe when they say, "Indifferent contemplative, and living happily"—he enters upon the third trance; when, through the abandonment of happiness, through the abandonment of misery, through the disappearance of all antecedent gladness and grief, he enters upon the fourth trance, which has neither misery nor happiness, but is contemplation as refined by indifference, this, O priests, is called the discipline in elevated concentration.

3.—Translated from the Aṅguttara-Nikāya (ii. 3^{10})

What advantage, O priests, is gained by training in quiescence? The thoughts are trained. And what advantage is gained by the training of the thoughts? Passion is abandoned.

THE CONVERSION OF ANIMALS

[REFLECTION ON THE BUDDHA]

Translated from the Visuddhi-Magga (chap. vii.)

THE Blessed One, moreover, was The Teacher, because he gave instruction also to animals. These, by listening to the Doctrine of The Blessed One, became destined to conversion, and in the second or third existence would enter the Paths. The frog who became a god is an illustration.

As tradition relates, The Blessed One was teaching the Doctrine to the inhabitants of the town of Campā, on the banks of Lake Gaggarā; and a certain frog, at the sound of The Blessed One's voice, obtained the mental reflex. And a certain cowherd, as he stood leaning on his staff, pinned him down fast by the head. The frog straightway died, and like a person awaking from sleep, he was reborn in the Heaven of the Thirty-three, in a golden palace twelve leagues in length. And when he beheld himself surrounded by throngs of houris, he began to consider: "To think that I should be born here! I wonder what ever I did to bring me here."And he could perceive nothing else than that he had obtained the mental reflex at the sound of the voice of The Blessed One. And straightway he came with his palace, and worshiped at the feet of The Blessed One. And The Blessed One asked him:—

> "Who is it worships at my feet,
> And flames with glorious, magic power,
> And in such sweet and winning guise,
> Lights up the quarters all around?"

"A frog was I in former times,
And wandered in the waters free,
And while I listened to thy Law,
A cowherd crushed me, and I died."

Then The Blessed One taught him the Doctrine, and the conversion of eighty-four thousand living beings took place. And the frog, who had become a god, became established in the fruit of conversion, and with a pleased smile on his face departed.

LOVE FOR ANIMALS
[SUBLIME STATE OF FRIENDLINESS]

Translated from the Culla-Vagga (v. 6.).

NOW at that time a certain priest had been killed by the bite of a snake, and when they announced the matter to The Blessed One, he said:

"Surely now, O priests, that priest never suffused the four royal families of the snakes with his friendliness. For if, O priests, that priest had suffused the four royal families of the snakes with his friendliness, that priest, O priests, would not have been killed by the bite of a snake. And what are the four royal families of the snakes? The Virūpakkhas are a royal family of snakes; the Erāpathas are a royal family of snakes; the Chabyāputtas are a royal family of snakes; the Kanhāgotamakas are a royal family of snakes. Surely, now, O priests, that priest did not suffuse the four royal families of the snakes with his friendliness. For surely, O priests, if that priest had suffused the four royal families of the snakes with his friendliness, that priest, O priests, would not have been killed by the bite of a snake. I enjoin, O priests, that ye suffuse these four royal families of the snakes with your friendliness; and that ye sing a song of defence for your protection and safeguard. After this manner, O priests, shall ye sing:

> " 'Virūpakkhas, I love them all,
> The Erāpathas, too, I love,
> Chabyāputtas, I love them, too,
> And all Kanhāgotamakas.

" 'Creatures without feet have my love,
And likewise those that have two feet,
And those that have four feet I love,
And those, too, that have many feet.

" 'May those without feet harm me not,
And those with two feet cause no hurt;
May those with four feet harm me not,
Nor those who many feet possess.

" 'Let creatures all, all things that live,
All beings of whatever kind,
See nothing that will bode them ill!
May naught of evil come to them!

" 'Infinite is The Buddha, infinite the Doctrine, infinite the Order! Finite are creeping things: snakes, scorpions, centipedes, spiders, lizards, and mice! I have now made my protection, and sung my song of defence. Let all living beings retreat! I revere The Blessed One, and the seven Supreme Buddhas!' "